FIGURE

FIGURE IT OUT
100 PUZZLES

by

D. St. P. Barnard

with illustrations by the author

A PAN ORIGINAL

PAN BOOKS LTD : LONDON

First published in 1973 by Pan Books Ltd,
33 Tothill Street, London SW1

ISBN 0 330 23607 5

Made and printed in Great Britain by
Cox & Wyman Ltd, London, Reading and Fakenham

PUZZLES HARD AND EASY

None of the puzzles in this book could be called either childishly simple or impossibly difficult, but the puzzles do vary, both in type and in standard of difficulty.

Of course, what proves difficult to one reader may appear comparatively simple to another; so much depends on a solver's personal aptitudes and interests. However, having grappled successfully with a problem, the solver is entitled to know how well he has done by comparison with other solvers at large. For this reason I have assigned to each puzzle a credit-rating in the form of one to five stars which appears together with the solution at the back of the book. Fairly simple puzzles are awarded one star, more challenging ones two stars, and so on up to five stars for a really difficult puzzle. I call the stars 'credits' rather than 'scores' simply because I feel that puzzle-solving should be treated as fun, and not looked upon as some sort of competitive examination.

For the most part, the puzzles themselves have been selected from items which have appeared during the last fifteen years (under either my own name or one of my pseudonyms) in the columns of the *Observer*, the Scottish *Sunday Mail*, the Birmingham *Sunday Mercury*, the *Ayrshire Post*, the *Rhodesian Sunday Mail*, the *Cambridge Evening News*, *Today*, *Look and Learn*, *Everywoman*, *Annabel* and *She*. Some of the others were originally prepared for advertising projects, and a few have been specially written for this book in order to produce a balanced diet.

As in my previous books, I must once again thank those thousands of solvers throughout the world who, over the years have, through my mail-bag, taught me more about puzzles than I have ever been able to teach them.

D. St. P. B.

Cheltenham Spa

MARBLING

A: 'I have more marbles than you.'
B: 'Bet you haven't. Look for yourself.'
A: 'OK. So you have more marbles than I have. But I'm the better player. All I have to do is to win three marbles off you, then I'll have twice as many marbles as you.'
B: 'Just you try.'
A: 'All right. You're on!'
B: 'Better player you call yourself, do you? Well this time I won. See!'
A: 'You won only two.'
B: 'So what? I have three times as many marbles as you have now.'
A: 'Play you again.'
B: 'All right.'
A: 'Aw, gee! You have all the luck.'
B: 'Now you haven't got any and I have . . .'
How many?

TANGLED TOTALS

Fig 1 shows three 5s, three 7s, and three 9s, arranged in ten lines, each line containing three of the numbers.

At present some of the lines add up to different totals. For instance $5 + 7 + 9 = 21$, while $5 + 5 + 5 = 15$, and $9 + 9 + 9 = 27$.

Can you rearrange the given numbers in such a way that every one of the ten lines adds up to the same total?

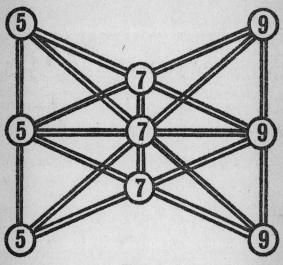

Figure 1

SPACE FREIGHT

The Space Freight Officer ran his eye down the list of containerized items requisitioned by ORBITER 99.

Item	lb wt	Item	lb wt
Drinking water	28	Batteries	61
Food	35	Colour TV	63
Fuel	42	Magazines	77
Camera	44	Bingo cards	84
Telescope	48	Beer	88

'That comes to just 570 lb,' he murmured. 'Now a Thermidor will take a pay-load of 180 lb, a Black Streak Mk II carries 190 lb, and a Woomera 200 lb; so by using one rocket of each type we shall be able to get all the stuff up to them without any pay-load wastage. The only problem seems to be deciding which items should be assigned to each of the three rockets.'

Can you help him?

LUCKY STRIKE

'There's gold in them thar 'ills,' said Jem.

'Ahhr,' said Jake.

'Aw,' said Joffy.

And Jem was right. Gold there was; nuggets for the picking up. Fig 2 shows their haul for the first week, with the weight in ounces marked on each nugget.

Three nuggets each they found, and the total value of Jem's nuggets was just twice that of Jake's.

Which three nuggets were found by Joffy?

Figure 2

So well known are the four men and their dogs who went to mow a meadow, that it is an omission greatly to be deplored that the song nowhere reveals the names of those famous characters.

However, I do have it on good authority that the four mowers were Messrs Skipper, Raffles, Towser, and Pompey, and that their dogs also answered to these four names, but since it is inconceivable that a man would deliberately share his own name with his dog, we may take it for granted that no man owned a dog answering to the same name as himself.

I have also been told that the dog owned by Mr Raffles did not have the same name as the owner of the dog called Raffles; neither did the dog owned by Mr Skipper have the same name as the gentleman who owned Towser; neither did Mr Towser's dog have the same name as the owner of Pompey; nor did Mr Pompey own Raffles.

Who can say which man owned which dog?

(6)   FENCING

The dotted square in Fig 3 represents a field I am fencing with posts and rails.

Already I have completed three sides, and these have cost me altogether £40 for materials. The posts cost 25 pence each, the railing works out at a few pence per foot.

Clearly, the fourth side will cost a trifle less than the others, for both corner posts C and D are already standing.

But just how much will it cost to complete the fencing?

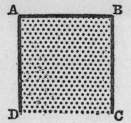

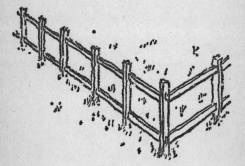

Figure 3

IN THE BALANCE

If you fancy yourself at weighing up the female form, try this one:

Figure 4

(8) WHAT PRICE YOUR WITS?

Some shopkeepers obligingly display their prices in big, bold figures. Others (jewellers and antique dealers seem to be the worst offenders) are so cagey that, even on their tiny tags they use a letter-code, which means that if you want to know the price you have to ask them.

The most popular sort of code used by secretive traders is based on choosing some ten-letter word or phrase, and assigning a number to each letter. For instance:

SOUTH WALES
1 2 3 4 5 6 7 8 9 0

Only the shopkeeper then knows that HA means 57p, or SH/OW means £15.26.

The other day I bought two items from a local antique shop. One was marked OF and the other T/EA. They came to a total of £6.41. My wife also bought two items, marked FB and I/RP for £5.69, while my daughter's two trinkets marked BT and LP totalled £1.77.

What code word does the dealer use for pricing his articles?

EN BLOC

Take a square block of wood 3 inches each way. Paint it black. Slice it into 1-inch cubes, and it will look like Fig 5.

The eight corner cubes will be black on three sides and the centre cube will show no black. Of the remaining twenty cubes twelve will be black on two sides and six black on only one side.

Notice that there are twice as many cubes black on two sides as there are cubes black on only one side, and there are eight times as many cubes black on three sides as there are cubes black on no sides.

I have a square block which is precisely the converse. When painted and cut into 1-inch cubes, there are twice as many cubes black on one side as there are cubes black on two sides, and there are eight times as many cubes black on no sides as there are cubes black on three sides.

What is the size of my block?

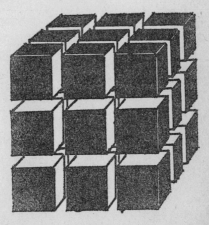

Figure 5

'I'm in a stew,' confessed the warder. 'There is a note here from PC Perkins to say that last night he arrested two rogues both in clerical garb. Well, when I came on duty this morning I found *three* fellows with their collars on back to front, and it now seems as though one of them is a genuine priest just visiting his lost sheep in jail. The trouble is, I don't know which is which.'

'Try asking them,' suggested the sergeant. 'The real priest can surely be relied on to tell the truth.'

'Yes, but I may be talking to the con-man who, Perkins says, is so inveterate a liar that he never tells the truth – while the card-sharp is a shifty fellow who sometimes lies and sometimes doesn't according to whether it suits him or not.'

The sergeant crossed to the cells.

'Who are you?' he asked the man in Cell One.

'The card-sharp,' replied the occupant, and the sergeant moved on to Cell Two.

'Who is the man in Cell One?' he asked.

'The con-man,' came the reply.

'Who do you say is in Cell One?' asked the sergeant turning to the occupant of Cell Three.

'The priest,' said the man in Cell Three.

'Obviously,' said the sergeant, turning to the warder, 'you had better release the chap in . . .'

Which cell?

The old Antoinette-style headboard looked bedraggled, and a satin remnant from the January sales seemed just the thing for re-covering it, but there remained the question of buttons for the quilting. Gold was Patricia's first preference, but the supplier had only ten gold buttons left in his stock.

'Gold and blue go well together,' he suggested. 'You could arrange them in some sort of pattern: ten gold buttons in five lines of four buttons each, and the rest blue, for instance.'

It was only when Patricia got home with her ten gold buttons and a dozen and a half blue ones that she realized what a headache it would be to follow the haberdasher's suggestion.

Fig 6 shows the arrangement of buttons on the quilting. Just where should the ten gold buttons be placed to form a symmetrical pattern in which it is possible to distinguish five straight lines each containing four gold buttons?

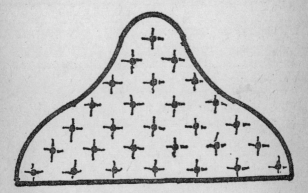

Figure 6

A 5 ft × 3 ft piece of tin sheeting seemed just the thing for making three square topless boxes for storing daffodil bulbs, so I commenced by pencilling out the sheet in one foot squares.

The heavy lines in Fig 7 show my first attempt at planning the cuts. The Z-shaped piece in the centre will fold into a box as shown in the diagram, but neither of the remaining two pieces can be folded into a box shape.

Can you discover how the sheet can be divided into three pieces, each of which can be folded (without further cutting) into a square topless box?

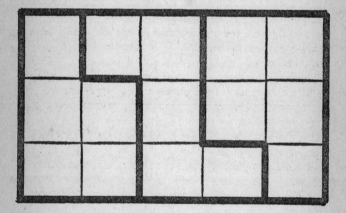

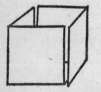

Figure 7

(13)   SUPER BLONDE

They have a super blonde at our Supermarket. She operates the cash register. Couldn't help noticing her as the queue of customers filed past.

'One bottle of tomato ketchup and a pound of sausages.' Clickety-click went the machine. 'Twenty-seven pence,' she chirped. Pretty voice she has.

'One packet of Bubblecrisps and a can of baked beans. Fourteen and a half pence, please.' Beautiful eyes.

'One pound of sausages and a jar of honey. Thirty-five and a half.' Good figure too.

'On baked beans and a bottle of tomato ketchup. Fifteen and a half pence.' Long, sensitive fingers she has.

'A jar of honey, and a packet of Bubblecrisps. That comes to twenty-eight and a half, please.' What a smile!

My turn now.

'Twenty-four pence,' she said sweetly. I raised my hat, fumbled in my pocket, dropped my change, and stumbled over the fat lady in front of me as I drifted, cloudlike, towards the door.

'One moment,' cried the sweet, angelic voice. 'You have forgotten your two purchases.'

'What two purchases?' I asked blankly – and then I remembered that I had bought a couple of items; same sort of things as the others had bought, but which two I just couldn't recall.

Can you?

'This Tinker, Tailor, Soldier, Sailor method of settling great questions of state is absolutely ridiculous,' complained the Chancellor. 'Fancy choosing a commander-in-chief by seating all the generals around the table and counting out every third man until only one remains.'

'It is the traditional method in Cryptonia,' sighed the Keeper of the Royal Shoe-laces.

'But what a tragedy for the country if the choice should fall on Gringoli,' groaned the Chancellor.

'The remedy is in your own hands,' replied the Keeper. 'Since you are responsible for seating the eight generals, place Gringoli as number Three, or number Six, or even as number One. You can then be sure of his being eliminated on the count.'

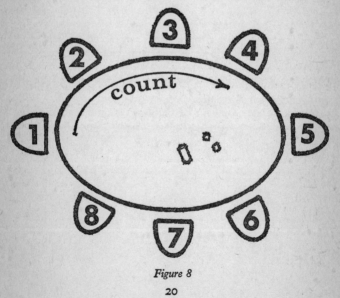

Figure 8

'Gringoli has foreseen that possibility,' sighed the Chancellor contemplating the plan of the table shown in Fig 8. 'He has now persuaded the King that, instead of counting out every third man, a pair of dice should be thrown *after* the generals have been seated, and that the total on the two dice should determine the span of the count. For instance, should the dice total 4, then every fourth man is to be dismissed. If the dice total 9, then every ninth man will be dismissed on each count until only one remains at the round table. Tell me – where should I seat Gringoli, for I cannot know what number the dice will show, and I am determined to eliminate the man?'

(15) TANGO

The three married couples were celebrating their triple-wedding anniversary at a dinner dance, and for most of the evening the husbands had partnered their wives. But no girl danced the tango with her husband. Instead Alex led Dorothy on to the floor. Brian partnered Charles' wife, and Florence's husband danced with Elizabeth.

To which girl was each man married, and with which girl did he dance the tango?

The distance we call a 'chain' got its name from the fact that, in former times, surveyors used real chain for measuring distances. The links of surveyors' chains were long ones, each measuring 7.92 inches.

I came across an odd length of surveyor's chain in a job lot I bought at an auction recently. It consisted of only nine links, and someone had joined the two ends together. I amused myself trying to discover how many differently proportioned triangles I could make by laying out the loop of chain in various ways. As Fig 9 shows, the answer turned out to be three.

What is the smallest number of links such a chain would have to contain in order to make ten triangles of different shapes?

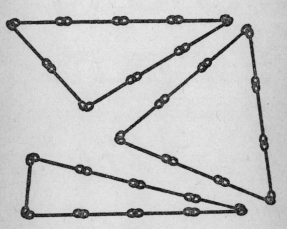

Figure 9

The diagram in Fig 10 shows five buttons, each bearing one of the digits 1 to 5. They have been arranged into two groups to represent a simple multiplication sum, the answer (or product) of which is 7,874.

Can you rearrange the five buttons into a multiplication sum which will produce a bigger product?

Come to think of it, what is the largest possible product it is possible to obtain by rearranging the buttons into two groups representing a multiplication?

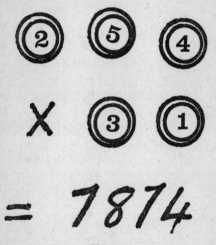

Figure 10

24

If I were to tell you that . . .

When the day before yesterday was referred to as 'the day after tomorrow', the day that was then called 'yesterday' was as far away from the day we now call 'tomorrow' as yesterday is from the day on which we shall be able to speak of last Monday as 'a week ago yesterday' . . .

On what day of the week would I be making that statement – assuming of course that I was speaking the truth?

'Sorry, but I am completely out of two-tier cakes,' said the pastrycook. 'Though, wait a minute! I have an idea. I have one square cake left. If I were to cut it up to form two square cakes the joins would never be noticed once the cakes have been iced.'

'Could it be done?' asked Mrs Motherbride.

'I think so. Shall we settle on two tiers, the lower tier having a side just twice the length of the top tier? It will be a tricky task of course, because to avoid crumbling I shall try to divide this original cake with the fewest possible number of cuts.'

Fig 11 is merely a square for you to ponder over. What is the smallest number of straight cuts necessary to achieve the pastrycook's proposal?

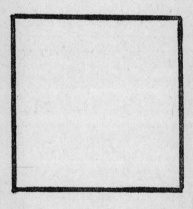

Figure 11

The village church at Summers Magna is, alas, a poor one. The old tattered set of hymn-board numbers is no longer serviceable, and the vicar has decided that he simply must buy a new set.

In order to buy as few cards as possible the vicar has decided that he will never use more than four hymns in any one service, nor ever use the same hymn more than once in a service.

Even so, because he is able to get only single-sided cards (ie, cards with a numeral printed on one side only) he has still to purchase quite a few in order to cater for all possible selections of hymn-numbers from the 779 hymns contained in the church hymnal.

However, cunningly he has noticed that, by turning the 6 upside down it can, if necessary, be made to serve as a 9 – and vice versa.

This reduces somewhat the number of cards he needs, but he is still a bit vague about exactly what selection of cards he should buy to cover all possible selections of four different hymns from the 779 in the hymnal.

Any suggestions?

Clearly it dated from the last century; no one but a Victorian would have decorated so commonplace a thing as a station noticeboard with such an ornate pattern of scrolls. I simply had to photograph it, and that photograph is now reproduced in Fig 12.

While waiting for my train I passed the time in trying to trace out words by following the white lines from one letter to the next. 'STREAMS' was the longest word I managed to discover when suddenly I found one word which used all thirteen letters, and even had the hyphen in the right place.

But what was more astonishing, this hyphenated 13-letter word even gave a clue to the possible identity of the board's designer.

Can you discover what the word is?

Figure 12

Fig 13 represents a geometrical figure known as 'The Sphinx'. It is a figure which lends itself to many interesting dissection problems, one of which is to divide the sphinx into four equal parts, each of which is itself a miniature sphinx.

It is quite a tricky problem.

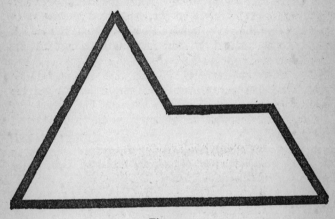

Figure 13

'It's like this,' explained Tom Tiley, the union secretary. 'The management say that there is no chance of meeting production schedules if we work less than the 44 hours a week we are putting in at present.'

'Then it's strike!' shouted Mullaley.

'So they have put up two alternative proposals,' continued Tom. 'If we like, they will cut the *official* working week to 40 hours, but we shall have to work 4 hours overtime to keep the schedule running, and for those four hours we shall be paid time-and-a-half.'

'Strike!' shouted Mullaley.

'The alternative plan,' went on Tom, 'is for the working week to stay at 44 hours with no overtime, but with an all-round rise of fivepence in the pound in the hourly rate of pay.'

'Strike!' shouted Mullaley.

'I have been doing a bit of figuring,' explained Tom, 'and it seems we shall be better off under . . .'

Which plan?

Fig 14 shows the insignia just adopted by the Black Diamond Club. It comprises a (gold) circle enclosing a (silver) rectangle, within which appears a black diamond.

The badge is 2 inches in diameter overall, and an argument has arisen in the club as to how long each side of the diamond is.

Can you decide the question for them?

The problem requires a bit of thought, but it needs no difficult geometrical formula to solve it.

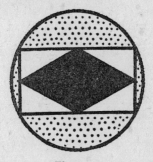

Figure 14

I do wish the Post Office would stop chopping and changing my telephone number. Maybe it has something to do with efficiency, but it is very annoying. Not only has one got to learn one's new number, but one also has to advise everyone (except one's creditors) that there has been a change of number.

But I mustn't complain too much. Things could have been worse. There are three things about my new number which makes it easier for me to remember. Firstly, both the old and new numbers each consist of four digits. Secondly, the new number is exactly four times the old number. Thirdly, the new number happens to be the old number written back to front.

So I should find little difficulty in remembering that it is . . .

Now what the dickens is it?

SET-UP

Here is a set-up which is easy enough to construct. All you really need to do is to rule six squares on a piece of paper, and then cut out five small squares of paper or card on which to write the letters S, E, T, U, P. If you are good with your hands, you may care to make a more permanent set-up as shown in Fig 15, but the paper version will serve adequately.

The five lettered squares should first be arranged as shown in the picture of the box.

Now comes the difficult bit.

Push the lettered squares around by sliding them one at a time into wherever the vacant space happens to be, until they spell out the words 'SET UP' as shown in the little diagram below the box.

With a bit of patience you should get it, but what is the smallest number of moves in which, starting from the arrangement shown, you can get yourself SET UP?

Figure 15

CAN BE DONE

The *Can Be Done* stall at the fair displays nine cans, each bearing a number, and stacked as shown in Fig 16.

A competitor is allowed three shots, and each shot must dislodge just one can; if a shot topples more than one it doesn't count.

For the first can to fall, the thrower scores the number shown on it. For the second fall he is credited with twice the number on the toppled can, and for the third fall he scores three times the can-number.

To win a prize the total score for all three shots must come to exactly FIFTY – no more and no less.

Which three cans should a competitor aim for, and in what order should he try to topple them?

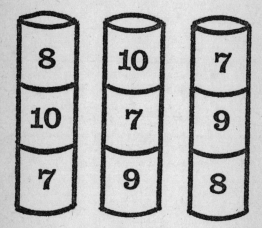

Figure 16

TINKER, TAILOR...

There are only six houses in Nursery Street, Rhymetown; three on one side, and three directly opposite them on the other. All six are inhabited by notorious characters.

The soldier has the tinker and Mr Davies as his next-door neighbours. The sailor lives next door to the thief, and Mr Eastley has one of the end houses. The beggarman lives directly opposite Mr Barlow, but Mr Foley does not live opposite the thief. The tailor and Mr Coutts are both neighbours of Anderson.

Can you tell which calling is followed by each of the six men?

(29) TUNNEL OF HORRORS

It was a rainy day at the fair-ground, and the Tunnel of Horrors offered at least one way of getting out of the rain, so we took our places in the little single-seater cars which clattered their endless way in through the banging doors, past the grotesquerie, and back out for a glimpse of reality before plunging again into the gloom.

Andy was the first to bag a car. By the time Barbara had paid her fare, seven more cars had passed, so she got the eighth car after Andy's. Then eight more cars passed before Cora got the ninth after Barbara's. Dora got the sixth car after Cora's, and Edward the fourth car after Dora's. Finally, I caught the eighth after Edward's.

And thus, if we didn't actually enjoy the horrors, we escaped the rain.

The first to get off was Rusty who was occupying the single car that separated me from Andy.

Rusty of course is the nickname of whom?

'How many girls are taking part?' asked the florist.

'Five,' said Uncle Thomas.

'Then may I suggest five bouquets of roses. Eight blooms to each bouquet would, I think, be appropriate. Now what about colour; yellow, pink, white, red?'

'Why not mix them?'

'That should be effective. Ten blooms of each colour will come to forty blooms, and for the sake of variety I shall make each of the bouquets contain a different proportion of colours – though I think we should include at least one rose of each colour in each bouquet.'

So it turned out that Alice received a bouquet which contained more yellows than all her other colours put together. Barbara had fewer pink than any other single colour. In Claire's bouquet, the total number of yellows and whites was the same as the total number of pinks and reds. Diana had twice as many whites as reds, and Effie's bouquet revealed an equal number of reds and pinks.

How many roses of each colour did each girl have in her bouquet?

Neat and accurate young Marmaduke tried to be with his homework, but on this occasion he was just putting his books and pens away when disaster occurred: the ink spilt and ran in an untidy blot right across one of his arithmetic exercises. Fig 17 shows the unhappy outcome.

Only three figures remained legible and, try as he might, young Marmaduke could not for the life of him remember what figures had been in the obliterated spaces. But he did manage to remember that, by an odd coincidence, the whole sum had contained each of the ten digits 0, 1, 2, 3, 4, 5, 6, 7, 8, 9.

Could you have restored the original sum for him?

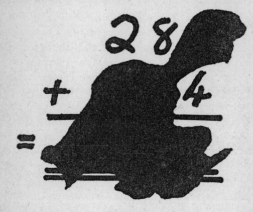

Figure 17

The hot midday sun was rising from the main street of Death Canyon as the seven rustlers swaggered out of the whisky-parlour, each to take up what he considered to be the best strategic position for the gun-battle which was soon to commence.

Andy, Billy, Charlie, Dick, Eddie, Ferd, and Gunnie were preparing to shoot it out, and the map in Fig 18 shows the positions they chose. As you can see, each man was in a position from which he could take a bead on just two of the others, and without budging from these spots the seven of them blazed away. Dick was the first to fall, plugged by a shot from Andy who was the sole survivor of that fearful day.

Who shot whom, and in what order did the victims fall?

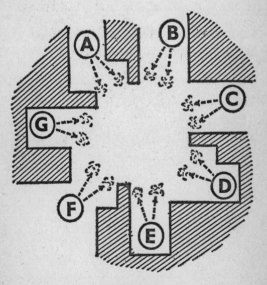

Figure 18

Most pencil and paper mazes are child's play, but this one should take quite a bit of solving.

Fig 19 shows a maze consisting of circles linked by paths. The idea is to start from one of the large, open, outer circles, and move along the paths to the Home circle in the centre.

The number on each circle tells how many steps you must take on your next move. For instance, if you were to start from the outer circle marked 2, your first move must then cover two steps, which will land you either on another 2 or on 6. According to which it is, you must then take two or six steps respectively for your next move.

Back tracking is permitted, but your last move must land you exactly in the Home circle. Through it and out again is not good enough.

There is only one way into the maze. It may be difficult to find, but once found it is very easy to remember. Can you discover it?

Figure 19

'What sort of response did we get to the staff advertisement?' asked the Personnel Manager peeling off his overcoat.

'Thirty-six replies altogether,' replied his secretary. 'All of them have at least one of the qualifications we listed, and some have all three. Twenty-five of the applicants can type, twenty can do shorthand, and twenty-one have some knowledge of book-keeping.'

'Let me see,' said the Personnel Manager running his finger down the figures which his secretary handed across. 'There are seven with typing and shorthand only, nine with typing and book-keeping only, and six with shorthand and book-keeping but no typing. I can't see them all. Better just make appointments for those girls who have all three qualifications.'

How many girls were invited for an interview?

WATERED DOWN

The dairyman was in a quandary. The demand for milk had
been heavy and now, just as he was about to shut up shop for
the day, two customers arrived – one with a half-gallon can,
and the other with a quart pot. And in the store was just enough
milk to fill the half-gallon can.

What to do?

To tell the quart-potter that he would have to do without
milk for his porridge would be unkind. To share the milk
equally between them would mean a disgruntled half-
galloner.

There was only one way to bring happiness and joy to both
his customers – surreptitiously to add enough water to satisfy
both of them. There was water to be had in abundance from the
tap, but he had started by filling the half-gallon can with milk,
and the only other measure available (apart from the second
customer's quart pot) was an empty three-pint jug.

The question was, how to add water in such a way that he
could give each customer the required quantity of liquid, while
making sure that the quality of richness was in each case the
same. After all, he didn't want one customer to get weaker milk
than the other, for he was a just and honest dairyman.

What was the most expeditious way of carrying out his
plan?

The metal plate shown in Fig 20 has an oddly shaped hole cut in it, and the piece which was removed was again divided into two smaller pieces.

Six odd bits of metal are shown below the main diagram. Which two of these were cut from the piece taken from the metal plate? Or, to put it another way, which two of the lettered bits could be fitted together to fill the hole in the plate?

The bits may be twisted around, but not turned over.

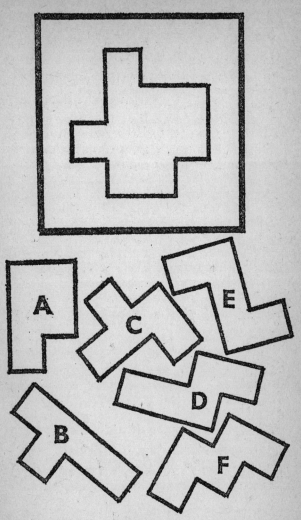

Figure 20

There are five single wards in the private wing of the Riddleton General Hospital. The Emergency Ward at the far right is at present free, but the other rooms are occupied by patients named Ayker, Bonybroke, Coffer, and Dyer. At present they are accommodated in the rooms indicated by the initials in Fig 21.

They seem happy enough, but the matron has taken it into her mind that Dyer should change places with Ayker, and Coffer with Bonybroke. You see, the matron has a very orderly mind, and all her patients would then be in neat alphabetical order ready to be filed.

Since all of them are private patients who have paid for their privacy, it is of course inconceivable that any two patients should be in the same room at the same time. Moreover, it is unthinkable that a patient should be left unattended in one of the draughty corridors while another is being moved.

What is the smallest number of moves in which the poor, harassed, unaided, junior nurse can carry out the matron's orders?

Figure 21

I have just been talking to Bill Motson. Bill is the secretary of our local social club which has planned to hire a coach next Saturday for a trip to the seaside.

He was just on his way back from visiting the bus company, because five more members had opted to join the party — making thirty-five all told, and originally he had booked a bus for only thirty.

'So you see,' said Bill, 'I had to go along and ask the company to let us have a bigger bus. Luckily they have a thirty-five seater available. It means of course that the club will have to pay an extra pound for the hire of the bigger bus.'

'Bad luck,' I said.

'Not at all,' said Bill. 'We are all sharing the cost between us, and the result of booking more people in the bigger bus means that we shall each have to pay tenpence less for the day's outing. The cost for each person is now only . . .'

How much?

(39)   CROSSNUMBER PUZZLE

A crossnumber is like a crossword, except that numbers instead
of words represent the answers which have to be inserted in the
squares. The clues too are, of course, numerical rather than
verbal.

CLUES

ACROSS

b. The sum of the digits in
   b dn.
d. A prime number.
e. *a dn* + *b ac* + *c dn*

DOWN

a. A palindromic number
   (ie, one which reads the
   same backwards as
   forwards)
b. 9 times *a dn.*
c. *d ac* multiplied by itself.

Can you discover the only set of numbers which will agree
with all these clues?

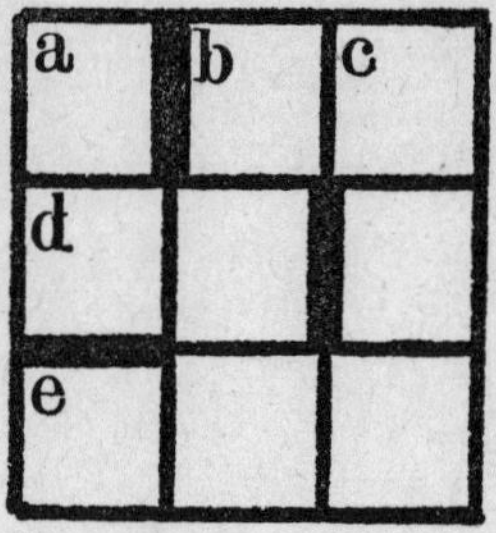

Figure 22

'That's annoying,' said Barbara looking at the Krispykorn packet.

'What's annoying?' asked Bertram, his eyes still glued to the sporting page.

'Well it says here:

BIG TWO-IN-ONE OFFERS

One Bath Towel with matching Hand Towel 35 coupons

One Hand Towel with matching Guest Towel 25 coupons

One Guest Towel with matching Face Flannel 15 coupons

One Bath Towel with matching Face Flannel

'It is the last pair that I really want, and the corner of the packet showing how many coupons are needed for the Bath Towel and Face Flannel has been torn off. How many coupons do you think the pair is worth?'

'No idea, but there's a horse called Face Flannel in the 3.30. I think I'll back him five bob each way.'

Could you have been more helpful in telling Barbara how many coupons she should send for the Bath Towel and Flannel?

The circle in Fig 23 contains eleven dots; the eight outer ones form a square, and the three inner ones form a triangle.

The problem is to draw straight lines right across the circle from circumference to circumference in such a way that the circle is divided into eleven areas – each area to contain just one dot, and no area to be without a dot.

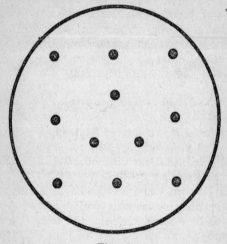

Figure 23

There has been a complaint from view-conscious residents about the allocation of the new Riddleston flats – a block of eight, arranged as shown in Fig 24.

The town surveyor, who has investigated the complaints, reports that twice as many people have a southward view (of the sewage farm) as there are people who can look eastward (to the gas-works). Those with a westward view (towards the housing estate) number only one-third of those who can look south, while the fortunate few who can look northward towards the downs number only half of those who can look east.

There are twenty souls in the block all told. How many occupy each flat, none of which is vacant?

Figure 24

WORD-CHAINS

The old word-chains so popular in Victorian times depended on changing the letters of one word to form another. The word-chains here are different – they depend on changing the *meanings* of the words. Thus TWENTY-SCORE-CUT-SNUB is a *meaningful* word-chain because twenty is a score, to score (with a knife) is to cut, and to cut (an acquaintance) is to snub him See how many of these ten word-chains you can complete:

1. ONLY	****	****	BLONDE
2. AUTUMN	****	****	JOURNEY
3. MARK	******	*****	ENTITLEMENT
4. TEACH	*****	*******	BEARING
5. COMPOST	*****	****	CLASS
6. JUMP	******	******	FLAVOUR
7. RESERVE	****	******	CAPACITY
8. DOWRY	*******	****	ROLE
9. DECLINE	******	******	OFFSPRING
10. SHILLING	***	*******	GRAVEL

The asterisks show the number of letters in the missing chain-words.

(44) GETTING OUT OF LINE

The twenty-five circles in Fig 25 carry, as you can see, five diamond-shaped counters lettered A, B, C, D, E.

The problem is to rearrange the counters by sliding them along the lines so that you finish up with no line (either horizontal, vertical, or diagonal) having on it more than one counter.

Provided you don't care how many moves you make the task is not very difficult, but it is quite a challenging problem to discover the smallest possible number of moves in which the desired result can be achieved.

Counters are not permitted to hop over one another when sliding along the lines. For instance, if you want to move counter D to Circle 2, it will mean that C will first have to be moved somewhere else.

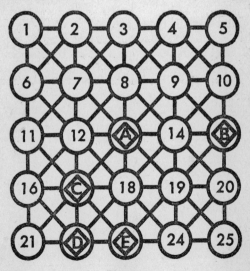

Figure 25

'So you have noticed the coincidence, eh?' said old Penny-whistle, the senior partner of Pennywhistle, Leacock, Mass-ingham, Norris, Oliphant & Sons.

'Though, of course,' he continued, 'it isn't really a coincidence at all. Actually, the five original members of the firm are all very old friends – together in the Army, you know; and it was my cousin Edward who suggested that when we got married we should each name our eldest son after one of the other chaps in the quintet. That is how young Leacock came to be called Archibald, and young Oliphant happens to be named Daffyd.'

'And now all five sons are in the business?'

'That is right. Norris named his son after young Edward's father, and Massingham's son is named after young Bertram's father.'

'And your own son?' I inquired.

'Ah, he's named after the father of young Cecil.'

Can you give the full name of each of the ten members of the firm consisting of the five fathers and five sons?

(46) CHERCHEZ LA FEMME

There always seems to be a woman in the case; the problem is to find her, and SHE sometimes lurks in unexpected places. For instance, can you find SHE in the letter-square shown in Fig 26?

By starting at any S, and moving left, right, up, or down to an adjoining H, and thence to an adjoining E, it is possible to spell out the word SHE in quite a number of different ways.

How many different ways can you discover?

E	H	S	H	E
H	E	H	E	H
S	H	S	H	S
H	E	H	E	H
E	H	S	H	E

Figure 26

'I found it,' said Wally.

'I pointed it out,' protested Frank.

'I picked it up,' declared George.

'We all looked for it,' said Leonard, 'so we should all stand in a ring and count eeni-meeni-myni-mo.'

'Not likely,' objected Quentin. 'Everyone knows that eeni-meeni-myni-mo always finish up with the sixteenth person to be counted, so Leonard will just start counting from sixteen places to his left.'

'Then I'll do the counting,' announced Victor, 'and whoever the last "mo" falls on will have to step out. Then we go on counting from that spot, round and round, until everybody has been counted out except one – and he'll be the winner.'

So they all stood in a ring as shown by Fig 27, and Victor did the counting.

And Victor won. So he got the penny they had found.

At which boy did Victor start counting his eeni-meeni-myni-mo?

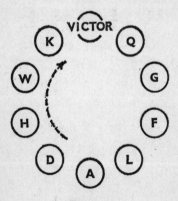

Figure 27

I used to smoke Mariner's Twist once upon a time, but I found it didn't quite suit my palate, so I began experimenting by mixing it with other brands.

I have now finally settled for a blend of three tobaccos: Mariner's Twist (which sells at 36p per ounce), Blarney's Flake (at 43p per ounce), and Three Zeros (at 45p per ounce).

All three brands are available in one-ounce tins, and I usually make up 1 lb of the mixture at a time. It suits me ideally, especially since the overall cost of my private blend works out at 39p per ounce, which is just about what I can afford to spend.

How many ounces of each brand do I buy to make up my 1 lb of mixture?

Whether or not you liked them at school, decimals do have real advantages over vulgar fractions; you can add, subtract, multiply, and divide decimals just like ordinary whole numbers. The only thing you have to be really careful about is to make sure that you get the decimal point in the right place in the answer. And in this problem even that has been done for you.

Fig 28 shows a division sum in which each of the numerals has been rubbed out and replaced by a question mark.

As you can see, the last line leaves no remainder.

What was the original sum?

One tip: remember that any figures brought down after the last decimal shown in the dividend must be noughts.

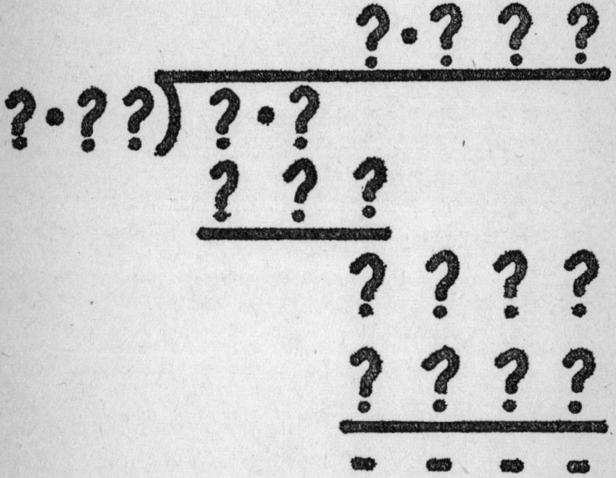

Figure 28

That something must be done to restore law and order to Neumania is obvious, and the Peace Committee has suggested an international 'police' force consisting of three contingents from the Northern powers (Atlantia, Battolia, Cornovia, Dubbland, and Empirea) and three from the Southern *bloc* (Voolubu, Womboland, Xandolia, Yubabi, and Zemberia).

But there agreement ends. The Northern powers will not agree to a force which includes both Womboland and Yubabi. The Southern *bloc* has retaliated by saying that it will not agree to contingents from both Atlantia and Dubbland.

Again, the Northern powers insist that, if both Voolubu and Womboland are included, then Zemberia should not also be represented. The Southern response to this is that, unless Womboland is represented, the *bloc* will not agree to both Cornovia and Dubbland. Moreover if Zemberia is excluded, the Southern *bloc* will not agree to the inclusion of Empirea.

If Zemberia is to send a contingent, then Battolia will refuse to join the force, while Xandolia has declared that she will withdraw if Cornovia is represented.

The conference is desperately seeking some suggestion as to how the peace force may be constituted in a way that will satisfy all parties.

Any suggestions?

PETROL AND PAINT

Fig 29 shows the new, spherical, 800,000 gallon petroleum gas container just installed by the Ooloolian Oil Company. The small container on the left is the old 100,000 gallon sphere.

The new one has yet to be painted. The small one, when it was installed required 20 gallons of paint to cover it, and the site manager now wants to know how many gallons of paint will be needed to give the new one a similar coat.

Any suggestions?

Figure 29

Solomon Golomb of the University of Southern California was
the man responsible for developing the game of Pentominoes
which consists of twelve differently shaped 'five-square domi-
noes', as shown in Fig 30. These twelve shapes may be fitted
together to form a great variety of patterns, and enthusiasts
keep on finding new ways of fitting the pieces together.

For instance:

Discard the three asterisked pentominoes, and use the remaining nine to form a larger version of the cross-shaped one.

It is a challenging problem for I find that it has only one
basic solution.

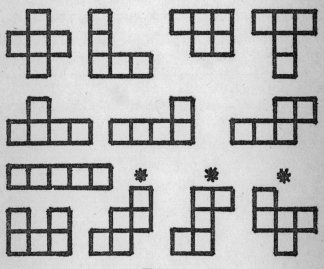

Figure 30

(53) BRIGHT AND EARLY

No doubt about some tradesmen having apt names. I once saw a butcher's shop called Hacker and Joynt. In Wales, so I am told, is a solicitor whose plate announces the name of Will Wrangle, and now in the newspaper I have just read of a pound-keeper called Penney.

Talking of newspapers reminds me of our local newsvendors who glory in the name of Bright & Early.

In the road where they start their morning deliveries there is the same number of houses on each side of the street. Bright is supposed to do one side, and Early the other. But since Bright is never early, Early starts off by doing the first five houses on Bright's side. Then when Bright turns up he takes over at the sixth house while Early crosses the road to begin his own deliveries.

But although Early is early he is not bright, so Bright (who is bright even if not early) finishes his own side well ahead of Early, whereupon he crosses the road to finish off the last nine houses on Early's side.

Clearly Bright makes more deliveries than Early, but how many more?

I call this game ROTAS for two reasons; the first is that the word '*rota*' is Latin for 'wheel', and the diagram in Fig 31 certainly looks something like wheels within wheels. The second reason we can leave for the moment.

The idea is to discover five letters which can be inserted into the five blank central circles so that, by starting at each of the sixteen letters on the outer circumference, and following the connecting lines in to the centre, it will be possible to spell out sixteen different four-letter English words.

What are the five letters needed in the centre?

Oh yes – I had almost forgotten to tell you the second reason for the name of the game. It is ... well, never mind; perhaps you can guess.

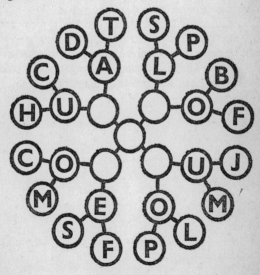

Figure 31

FLAT OUT

A newly completed maisonette block just around the corner consists of three floors with one flat on each.

The Warrens, who were first to move in, bagged the top flat, while the Mortons and Lewises tossed for choice of the other two.

The Mortons think it heavenly – no complaints from them – in fact, the only complaint from the entire block has come from Percy who wishes that the couple above him wouldn't take their bath quite so early, and thus disturb his sleep.

Apart from this, the three couples get on well together. On his way down in the morning, Roger usually calls in as he passes Jim's flat, and the two go off to work together. And about eleven, Catherine usually goes up to have a cup of tea with Mrs Lewis.

Absent-minded Norma finds the maisonette idea convenient, for it means that if she forgets something on her grocery order, she can pop down to Doris' flat and borrow whatever it is.

What are the Christian names and surnames of each of the married couples, and which flats do they occupy?

When old Jaggers, the local newsagent, advertised for a new paperboy he took on all five applicants, Albert, Bob, Charlie, David, and Edgar, for a week's trial.

Each day he religiously recorded the boys' daily sales with chalk on an old placard-board standing beside the back door of his shop and on Friday totted up the totals for the five days.

On Friday night it rained, and two trickles of water obliterated a dozen of the figures. Of the missing statistics all that the boys could remember was that on Wednesday Edgar had sold one copy more than Charlie had sold on Tuesday.

Fig 32 shows what remained of the record on Saturday morning, and old Jaggers promised the job to the lad who could restore the missing numbers so that all the totals added up correctly.

Could you have got the job?

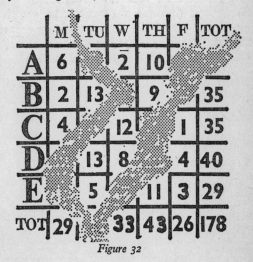

	M	TU	W	TH	F	TOT
A	6		2	10		
B	2	13		9		35
C	4		12		1	35
D		13	8		4	40
E		5		11	3	29
TOT	29		33	43	26	178

Figure 32

65

I have decided to smarten up my medicine chest by cladding it with white laminex, but laminex can be bought only in rectangular sheets – and it is expensive. The dimensions of the box are $9 \times 5 \times 4$ inches, as shown in Fig 33.

To cover the box completely I shall obviously need six pieces. What is the smallest single rectangular piece of laminex from which I can cut the six pieces with the minimum area of wastage?

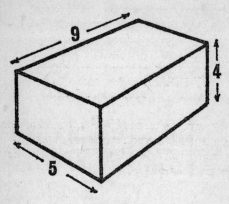

Figure 33

Calcularia has not yet adopted a decimal system of currency. It still uses three monetary units, something like Britain's erstwhile pounds, shillings, and pence – but in Calcularia the three units are called Sums, Bits, and Pieces.

Here as an example is a copy of a cash-register slip for some items a friend of mine brought back from a recent trip:

	Sums	Bits	Pieces
	3	7	5
	2	13	7
	7	6	7
	8	11	6
TOTAL	22	12	1

I know the addition looks all wrong, but I am assured that the cash register really did add up the prices correctly.

Can you tell how many Pieces to a Bit, and how many Bits to a Sum there are in Calcularia?

The local charity committee organized one of those motorized treasure-hunts last Saturday. All the cars were to assemble at Aixville, then from nine other villages in the area the competitors were to collect clues which, read jointly, would reveal where the barrel of beer was hidden in Zaxby.

First home to claim the barrel was young Wilkins. He must have planned his route very carefully because he managed to get from A to Z, collecting all his clues *en route* without visiting any village a second time. The rest of us seemed constantly to be going around in circles.

Fig 34 is a sketch map of the eleven villages involved showing the only available connecting roads.

What route did young Wilkins take?

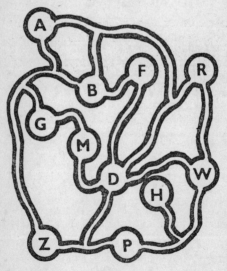

Figure 34

Albert and Bertie to represent the men, with Connie, Doris, and
Eve to represent the fairer sex; that is the set-up on our local
Charity Committee, and between them they share the offices of
President, Chairman, Vice-chairman, Secretary, and Treasu-
rer.

There was some discussion as to whether the Chairman
should be called a Chairwoman, because in fact she's a she (and
a very attractive young widow at that) but the traditional title
prevailed.

All five know each other well; indeed Albert and Eve are
twins, and Connie's husband is the Treasurer's brother. The
President and Treasurer have known each other from child-
hood. In fact they were in the same dormitory at boarding
school.

Romance too has its place on the Committee. The President
and Secretary are to be married next Saturday, with Doris in
attendance as matron of honour.

Can you name the holders of the five offices?

Dice used for the game of Crown and Anchor are marked, not with spots like ordinary dice, but with a Spade, a Heart, a Club, a Diamond, a Crown, and an Anchor – like the four identically manufactured dice shown in Fig 35.

In the mirror you can see reflected the tops of some of the dice. If the mirror were lowered a few inches, what symbol would you then see on the reverse side of each die, ie, the side at present facing away from you?

No guesswork is needed; the whole thing can be reasoned out. For instance, by studying the first and third dice, you can deduce that neither the Anchor nor the Diamond is marked on the side opposite the Club. See if you can take over the job of puzzling out the rest from there.

Figure 35

The only thing in the waiting-room was a pamphlet left behind by some other rail traveller, but since it was written in Norwedish it held out little promise of entertainment. But the page-numbers seemed to be written in English, so I whiled away the time by counting them up:

'One and two make three, and three make six, and four make ten ...' and so on, until I arrived at a final total of ninety. However, during the course of my laborious computation I happened to notice that someone had torn a leaf from the pamphlet, a leaf which of course would have borne two page-numbers not included in my addition.

How many pages were in the pamphlet originally, and which page-numbers had been torn out?

Many old puzzle books tell of travellers cutting up gold chains as security for board and lodging at some remote inn, but they seem to ignore the problem of joining the links together again.

One problematical traveller, on redeeming as much as he could afford of his chain, was left with thirty-five links in seven lengths as shown in Fig 36.

He was dismayed when the jeweller demanded $87\frac{1}{2}$ pence to repair the chain.

'I charge $2\frac{1}{2}$ pence to cut a link, and tenpence to weld it together again,' explained the jeweller. 'To join these seven pieces will clearly need seven cuts and seven welds – and that comes to $87\frac{1}{2}$ pence. No?'

No!

At $2\frac{1}{2}$ pence per cut and tenpence per weld, can you think of a cheaper way to join the seven pieces into an endless chain?

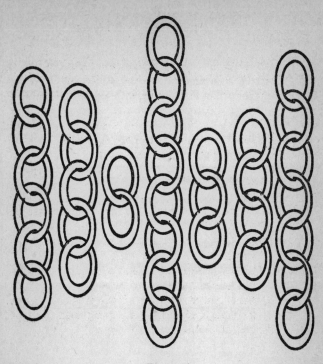

Figure 36

Fig 37 shows a partly completed crossword pattern. As it stands the pattern is asymmetrical, whereas the compiler of the puzzle wants the pattern to finish up with a balanced design – so that it will look the same, irrespective of which side it is viewed from.

What is the smallest number of black squares which must be added to the pattern in order to achieve the result?

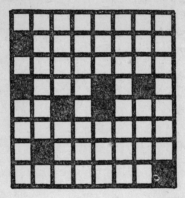

Figure 37

(65)   THE APPLE PIE MYSTERY

Half the apple pie was missing. But who had eaten it? That was the question mother put.

'Elaine didn't take it,' volunteered Albert who is very keen on Elaine.

'And I know Diane didn't take it,' put in Billy.

'Billy took it himself,' said Charles gruffly.

'Diane took it,' volunteered Elaine.

'Anyway, Albert didn't take it,' said Diane, smiling sweetly at Albert – which of course made Billy very angry.

Clearly someone must be lying.

As it so turned out, mother did ultimately discover that four of the five children had, in fact, spoken the truth. Only one of the statements made was a falsehood.

Which of the five had stolen the apple pie?

Fig 38 shows the cross-section of a novel garden-roller which a friend of mine purchased recently. In addition to the heavy (dotted) outer casing, there is a small cylinder (shaded in the diagram) which is free to roll around inside. The idea is that the weight of the small cylinder prevents the roller from over-shooting its mark. The circumferences of the various parts are marked on the diagram.

Personally, I have my doubts about the effectiveness of the contraption, but that is beside the point. What I should like to know is how many revolutions will the small 24-inch cylinder make if the roller is pushed a distance of 60 feet?

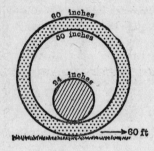

Figure 38

There is one kind of Bingo that goes by the name of 'Jackpot'. The idea is to fill, not the whole card or any line upon it, but merely a selection of numbers that will add up to exactly 100. If no one gets the exact total, the stakes are added to the next round – hence the name.

To get exactly 100 is rather more difficult than one may imagine; indeed it is not all that easy to discover a set of numbers that will total exactly 100.

For instance, what numbers on the card shown in Fig 39 would have to be covered if they are to total exactly 100 – no more and no less?

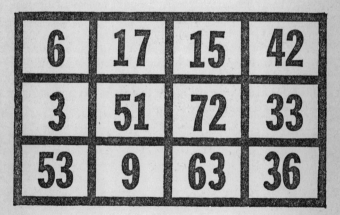

Figure 39

President Puzzooloo has just acquired a navy for the defence of his island republic. The new navy consists of two Houssa-class gun-boats. Unhappily their fuel consumption is somewhat excessive, and they can carry only enough wood to keep their boilers going for 24 hours (which gets them just 120 miles).

Puzzooloo is planning a grand voyage right round the island to show off the flagship, but his Lord High Grand Admiral has pointed out that the circumference of the island is considerably more than 120 miles – which is a matter of pride for Puzzooloo, but a headache for the Lord High Grand Admiral.

However, the Professor of Mathematics and Voodoo at the local university has calculated that, by using one vessel to refuel the other while at sea, the circumnavigatory voyage can be completed. Moreover, although it takes 8 hours for a gun-boat to refuel in port, at no time will either vessel have to ride in wait for its sister-ship to catch up with it. Only while actually transferring fuel at sea will Puzzooloo's stately progress be delayed. If the island were any bigger this would be impossible.

What is the circumference of the island?

Figure 40 shows four pieces of cardboard fitted together to form an irregular figure.

What is the smallest number of these pieces you would have to move in order to rearrange the figure into the form of a rectangle?

The answer is surprisingly simple, yet it may take quite a deal of spotting.

Figure 40

'It is just that I like to be sure,' said Quaddle as he fished a ruler from his pocket and squatted down beside the hotel dining table so that he could measure vertically how much wine was left in the decanter. It was a conical flask with the cork reaching down to just where the cone branched out, as shown in Fig 41.

'Two inches,' he announced. 'Just enough for this evening's dinner. And the height from the base to the cork is eleven inches, while the base itself is – oh! It doesn't come out very neatly in inches, but it has a diameter of . . .' He turned the ruler over. 'Of exactly twenty-four centimetres, while the base of the cork is two centimetres.'

'What on earth do you want to know all that for?' I asked.

'In case they try to swap decanters on us of course,' replied Quaddle.

'You will be wanting to measure it upside down next.'

'No need,' said Quaddle airily. 'The depth of wine in the decanter would then be . . .'

How many inches?

(In case you haven't a metric conversion table, a close enough approximation for the purpose of the problem is 1 cm = approximately 0.393700792598425203149606063 . . . inches.)

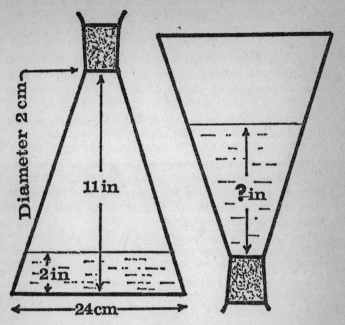

Figure 41

MISSING LINKS

Only within the last year has Euclidia overcome its repugnance to the telephone, but much remains to be done. At present only six towns in the country can boast a telephone service, and the links between these are anything but complete.

Alphalpha, the capital, is connected to all the other five towns, but Beetonia is connected to only four. Gammalia too is connected to four, whereas Deltata, Epsilonna, and Zetalena are each connected to only three towns.

It will be at least another two years before a proper exchange system will enable calls to be 'fed through' one town to another. In the meantime, it is possible to call one town from another only if a direct line connects them.

Thus although it is possible to make a call from Deltata to Zetalena, the only towns one can call from Epsilonna are – what?

THERE'S A TWIST TO IT

At first glance this puzzle may look ridiculously easy, but there is a twist to it which makes it rather a tricky question.

Imagine you have a set of cards, numbered as shown in Fig 42. These cards may be divided into groups in several different ways. For instance, if we want two groups, one of which is to be twice the value of the other, we could put cards 1, 2, 5, 7 (= 15) on one side, and 3, 4, 6, 8, 9 (= 30) on the other.

Now try to divide the cards into two groups (again with four cards in one group and five in the other) so that the sum of the figures shown on the cards in one group is *three* times the sum of the other group.

If your first attempt proves to be unsuccessful, remember you are dealing cards.

Figure 42

That is what the chalked-up notice outside the second-hand shop said – 'Eksepshunal Bargins'. And below this eye-catching announcement were listed the offers to which it referred:

Oil painting (jenuin)	70p
Brass bedsted	£4
Lectric ion (works)	60p
Bike (with pump)	£2·10
Weelbarrow (neerly new)	£3·05
Tipe riter (no E)	£2·80

Harry Treadfoot may not be able to spell, but apparently he knows how to sell, for five of the six items had been struck through.

'Business brisk?' I asked.

'Not bad,' replied Harry. 'Bit slow at first, but this afternoon the takings have been exactly twice what they were this morning.'

'Even better than that,' said I, 'for that remaining item is just what I have been looking for. I'll take it.'

Which item did I buy?

The top half of Fig 43 shows six numbered cheeses stacked on a cheese board marked A. Two other boards, B and C, are vacant.

The cheeses are to be moved one at a time from board to board until ultimately they are stacked two to a board in the order shown in the bottom half of the diagram.

There is one important proviso: at no time during the procedure must any cheese rest on another which bears a lower number than itself.

See how quickly you can do it.

You may be surprised to find just how long a job it proves to be.

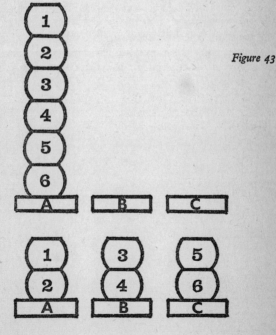

Figure 43

Fig 44 shows eight circles, on seven of which are white discs
bearing the letters G-L-A-S-G-O-W.

As they stand the name is spelt backwards, ie, it has to be
read in an anti-clockwise direction.

The object of the puzzle is to move the discs one at a time
so that the word GLASGOW can be read in its proper
(clockwise) direction.

A disc is permitted either:

(a) To move one space (either way) to an adjacent circle if
that circle happens to be free, or

(b) Jump over one disc to a vacant circle immediately
beyond it.

Thus the task could be accomplished by moving the discs in
the following order: LSOGAOGAWAGSOWGSO, but
this means seventeen moves in all.

Can you solve the problem in fewer moves than this? It does
not matter at what point the name starts, so long as it can be
read clockwise.

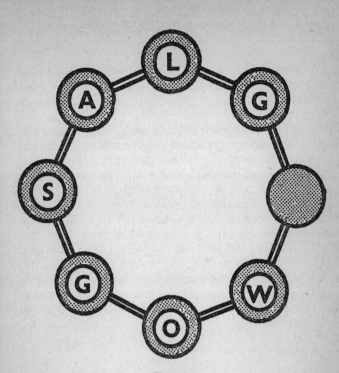

Figure 44

Some numbers have rather peculiar properties. All those referred to here are two-digit numbers. See how many of them you can find:

    a. Find a number whose double exceeds its half by 99.

    b. Find a number which is twice the product of its digits.

    c. Find a number which is thrice the sum of its digits.

    d. Find a number whose half exceeds its third by the sum of its digits.

    e. Find a number which is increased by one-fifth of its value if the order of its digits is reversed.

    f. Find a number which can be multiplied by itself simply by sandwiching an extra two digits in between its original two.

    g. Find a number which differs from its reverse by twice the product of its digits.

    h. Find a number the product of whose digits is twice the sum of its digits.

    i. Find a number which, if turned upside down, will be increased by 12.

WAKEY, WAKEY

It was while spending a week at Bournemouth last summer that I started thinking about the beautiful and stately symmetry of a vessel's wake. A friend took us out into the Channel for a day in his speed-boat, and we were running due South when a large ocean-going liner heading West crossed our course. She was dead ahead of us at the stroke of noon.

Six minutes later we took a bit of a tossing as we breasted the landward arm of the big liner's wake, and a short time later we crossed the other arm of her wake sweeping on its way out to sea.

Now by a strange coincidence we crossed that second arm of the wake at exactly the same time that the first arm would have reached us if, at noon, we had been anchored instead of heading South.

Can you say at what time we crossed the second arm?

Now don't start reaching for books on calculus. The reasoning behind the solution to this problem may be a trifle elusive, but the actual figuring required is extremely simple.

Wakey, wakey!

Perhaps it is because he reads murder yarns in his sitting-room every evening that Grandpa is obsessed by thoughts of burglars. When he has finished his nightly thriller he sets off for bed, going through all the seven doors of his bungalow, locking each one behind him as he goes.

At least, that is the theory. In fact, he invariably manages to lock himself away from the bedroom – which is where he wants to finish up.

Fig 45 shows a plan of Grandpa's bungalow. Try touring it yourself with a pencil, and you will appreciate his difficulty when you discover that there just is no way of reaching the bedroom from the sitting-room by passing once only through each of the seven doors.

If Grandpa is to make his nightly tour of inspection without doubling back on his tracks, an extra door will have to be made somewhere – but between where and where should that eighth door be built?

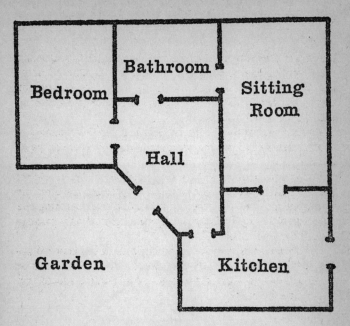

Figure 45

91

As a geometrical figure the pentacle (or five-pointed star) has so many interesting features that it has become intimately associated with black magic. If its five points are joined so that it becomes enclosed in a pentagon, its intricacies are even more fascinating – for, as Fig 46 shows, an enormous number of differently shaped figures can be discerned.

Consider for instance just the triangles in that figure. How many triangles can you distinguish? I hazard a guess that you will be surprised to find just how many there are. In the drawing, three triangles have been shaded to show the sort of unexpected shapes to look for. Counting the triangles is a far trickier business than it may appear at first sight.

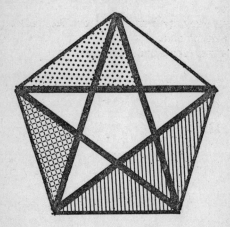

Figure 46

During the time that Britain was changing over from the old
£sd system to the new decimal coinage, slot machines created
quite a problem.

I remember that the cigarette machine at the corner needed
tenpenny pieces, and the local car park barrier operated with
fivepenny pieces. But the public telephone still swallowed nothing but old sixpences (which, as everyone was supposed to
know, were equal to two and a half pence).

I recall one occasion when, bearing these things in mind, I
asked the post-mistress to change a pound note for me.

'How would you like it?' she asked.

'Tenpennies, fivepennies, and sixpences,' I replied. 'Some of
each, please.'

And she obliged by counting out thirteen coins in exchange
for my one pound note.

How many of each coin did I receive?

HEART STRINGS

Who knoweth the ways of a woman's heart?

That is a question which has baffled philosophers ever since the first of them got jilted for treating his lady-love to a juicy sabre-tooth steak instead of a shiny sabre-skin coat. Any man who prides himself on his ability to play on the heart strings of the fair sex should try contemplating Fig 47.

Starting from some point on the heart, trace out the whole design without lifting pencil from paper, and without going back over any line a second time.

It is not as simple as it may look, but then involvements of the heart never are.

Figure 47

NUCLEAR PILE

Terribly dangerous stuff uranium! Put too much together in a lump and up it goes, taking half the surrounding countryside with it. So they keep it in canisters like the ones shown in Fig 48.

The number on the lid of each canister shows the strength of the uranium it contains, and the grey shaded parts are lead shielding. However, this particular pile is in danger of 'going critical' at any moment, because if three canisters are in a line, their total strength must not be more than 30 units. As it is, the top row (13, 6, 14), the middle-row (6, 10, 17) and the diagonal line (14, 10, 9) are all three units over the safety limit.

Clearly the canisters should be rearranged, but what is the smallest number of canisters which must be moved in order to make the pile safe, ie, to ensure that no single line of canisters (horizontal, vertical or diagonal) exceeds 30 units in total strength?

Figure 48

Last Monday the 9.00 AM train which I took from Aixville to Ceaview averaged 40 mph over the whole journey, though it was considerably slower than that while climbing the mountains.

My return journey by the 9.00 AM from Ceaview to Aixville on Tuesday averaged 60 mph, despite a long stop at Beatown, which is exactly halfway.

Can I say with absolute certainty:

a. That the average speed for the double journey was 50 mph?

b. That on Tuesday the average speed from Ceaview to Beatown was more than 30 mph?

c. That on Monday I reached Beatown later in the day than I reached that place on Tuesday?

d. That at some time on Tuesday I passed some spot at precisely the same time of day that I had passed that spot on Monday?

She takes quite a bit of figuring out does our Annabel. Just look at her in Fig 49.

Each of the five different letters of her name represents one of the digits 0 to 9. For instance, if A = 1, N = 2, B = 3, E = 4, L = 5, the sum would read 122 × 1 = 345. Unfortunately 122 × 1 does not equal 345, so that can't be right.

Can you discover which digit must be assigned to each of the five letters if the multiplication is to work out correctly?

There is only one possible solution.

Figure 49

'The Barton Bells, Brummidge, and step on it,' said Sir Withers Willington-Wills as he eased his gouty leg into the limousine. 'I want to be there by six.'

'Certainly, sir,' said the chauffeur, 'but there is no real need to hurry, sir. I have looked up the route, and provided we average thirty miles an hour we shall be there with half an hour to spare.'

'No, I don't want that,' growled Sir Withers. 'Nothing I hate more than arriving at a function early. Better make it twenty miles an hour instead.'

'That, sir,' said the chauffeur, tucking a warm woolly blanket around his employer's tender limb, 'would mean arriving half an hour late.'

'Would it now? Then just drive at such a speed as will get us there on the dot of six.'

'Certainly sir.'

And the efficient Charles drove off at . . . what speed?

That round table at which King Arthur seated his knights must
surely have been a gigantic piece of furniture, for most authori-
ties put the number of knights at King Arthur's court at one
hundred and fifty.

Maybe the giant table was used only for special festivities,
and on less formal occasions Arthur may have used a somewhat
smaller version just big enough to accommodate himself and
his six cronies, Bedivere, Galahad, Launcelot, Merlin, Percival,
and Tor – as shown in Fig 50.

Now suppose that for the sake of good comradeship, these
seven decided that no man should have the same neighbour on
more than one occasion during the month – thus for instance,
after the arrangement shown in the diagram, Arthur must not
again be seated next to either Bedivere or Tor. On how many
days in the month could the seven dine together at the round
table subject to that rule?

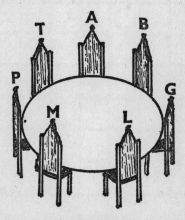

Figure 50

Four counters or buttons, and a sheet of paper ruled into squares as shown in Fig 51 are all that one needs for this problem.

The general idea is to place the four counters on the paper in such a way that every one of the 49 squares is in line (either laterally or diagonally) with at least one counter. At first glance this may seem almost impossible, but the diagram shows one arrangement which almost does the trick. Here every single square, with the sole exception of the one that is asterisked, is in line with some counter.

Leaving the black counter where it is, can you move the other three into new positions so that every single square is in line (laterally or diagonally) with at least one counter?

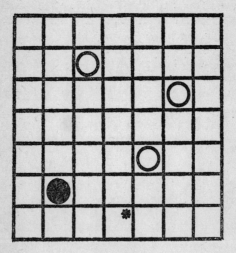

Figure 51

'If Tom can fill a tank with water in ten minutes . . .'

'Don't go on. I know that one.'

'No you don't. If Tom can fill it in ten minutes, and Bill can fill it in four minutes . . .'

'Then in one minute Tom can fill one-tenth, and Bill can fill one-quarter, so together they fill seven-twentieths in one minute, and will need two and six-seventh minutes to do the job.'

'Wrong! You didn't wait for me to explain that Bill works twice as fast as Tom.'

'Hang on! That's impossible! If Bill works twice as fast as Tom, he would fill the tank in five minutes not four.'

'Wrong again. You see, the bottom of the tank has a leak in it, so Bill has to cope with only four minutes' leakage, while Tom has ten minutes' leakage to contend with. Anyway, I don't want to know how long it will take them to fill it. All I want to know is how long will it take the water to leak away after the tank has been filled?'

Figure 52

IF

AND

AND

WHAT

will be the outcome of a tug-o'-war between a mother and two boys pitted against a father and three girls?

STEPPING IT UP

No doubt about it; escalators can speed things up. The only trouble with them is that I feel rather goofy just standing there and being carried up like a tin duck at a shooting gallery. So I usually try to look intelligent by occupying my mind with such questions as how fast escalators go and why women wear stiletto heels.

I timed my journey the other day, and found that if I stepped aboard the escalator and let it carry me up, the journey took exactly half a minute. On the other hand, if I stepped on and walked up while the escalator was travelling, I could cut the time to 12 seconds.

All this was fine, but yesterday the escalator broke down, and I had to walk up the stationary steps pedestrian fashion.

How long did it then take me to reach the top?

One of the oldest puzzles known consists of nine dots arranged in the form of a 3 × 3 square. The solver is required to strike out all nine dots with just four consecutive strokes (ie, four straight lines drawn without removing the pencil from the paper). The answer is so well known that I refrain from reproducing it, but how about the twenty-five dots shown in Fig 53?

What is the smallest number of consecutive strokes needed to strike through all of these dots?

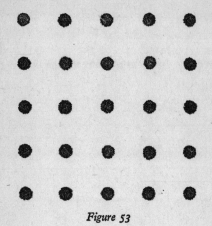

Figure 53

(92)   FITTING NUMBERS

Fig 54 shows the outline of a multiplication sum from which all the numbers have been removed – or perhaps I should say 'from which the first six numbers have been removed', because the original sum consisted of the digits 1, 2, 3, 4, 5, 6.

Can you replace those six digits in such a way that the original sum is restored?

It is a tricky little problem, for there is only one way in which the numbers 1 to 6 can be arranged if the sum is to work out properly.

Figure 54

'How is work progressing?' asked the managing director of the building firm.

'Not very fast,' sighed the foreman. 'The bricklayers have just handed me a new demand.'

'But it was only last month that they held a stop-work meeting and decided to reduce the daily output of each man by one hundred bricks. We had to put on two extra bricklayers to keep up normal production. What are they after this time?'

'The same again. They have decided that the darg should again be reduced for each man by one hundred bricks a day.'

'Well we must keep up the rate of building,' said the managing director. 'I suppose there is nothing for it but to engage another two layers.'

'With the new darg I am afraid that won't be enough,' said the foreman. 'I have been working it out. To keep the rate of production steady we shall have to engage another three men this time.'

'How many bricklayers will then be on the job?'

Can you answer the managing director's question?

TABLE TOP

When the proprietor of the Three Tuns Tavern decided to close his beer garden in favour of a verandah restaurant, the wooden tables from the garden created a problem. They were 2 ft 6 in square, but (as shown in Fig 55) each had a 6-inch round hole cut in the centre to accommodate the large sunshades he used to put up on hot days.

Now a hole may be acceptable in a garden table, but one can hardly expect diners in a restaurant to risk losing their bottle of champagne down a hole.

In what way can the garden table be cut into the smallest possible number of parts, and with the minimum wastage of wood, so that the parts can be jig-sawed together to form a rectangular table-top with no hole in it?

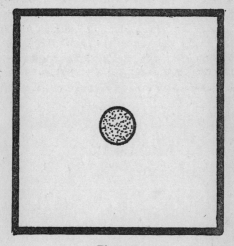

Figure 55

Now that the white pawns have revolted and overthrown their aristocratic court, they face the question of land distribution. Justice demands that their half of the board should be distributed amongst the pawnitariat in such a way that each pawn receives a plot containing the same number of squares, and of *exactly the same shape*, as all the others. But a problem has arisen because no pawn is prepared to move from the square he now occupies. The entire revolution is therefore in danger unless someone can show how the land should be divided.

Fig 56 shows the present disposition of the pawns, and suggestions as to how the land should be divided so that each pawn occupies an equal area of the same shape would be welcome. But please do not try to claim that shapes like (a) and (b) in the diagram are 'the same'. However much you rotate them, these two shapes will always be the reverse of one another, and reversionism is punishable *en passant* under the new regime.

You may notice that, under the Departheidization Act, all colour discrimination of squares has been abolished as a gesture of pawnitarian support for their black brothers still languishing under a feudal yoke on the other side of the board, but this is quite incidental.

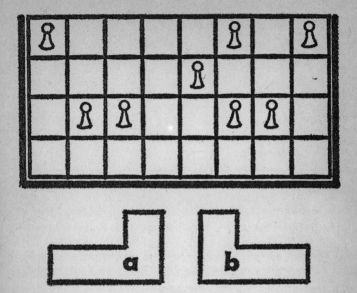

Figure 56

There is a very old problem about a wall-climbing snail that goes something like this:

Confronted by an 11-foot high slippery brick wall, a snail begins to climb it. In one hour of climbing he manages to get up 5 feet, but at the end of every hour's climb he rests for an hour. During this hour's rest, he slips back 3 feet. How long will he take to climb the wall?

One is tempted to say that since his effective rate of climb is only 2 feet in 2 hours, he will take 11 hours to climb an 11-foot wall, but of course this is wrong. True – at the end of the sixth hour he is only 6 feet up, but the 5 feet he will climb in the next hour will see him safely perched on top of the wall. So the total climb takes 7 hours.

So much for the old puzzle. Now for the new bit.

Working the same routine of one hour's steady effort followed by one hour's rest, how long should it take the snail to descend the other slippery side of the same slippery wall?

Be warned! This is a far more subtle question than the first. Not one person in fifty is likely to get it right.

The king of Neumania was furious. It had taken him weeks to design a royal standard for himself, and now that the first of the new flags had been unpacked it looked like Fig 57.

The king's instructions had been clear enough: a crown in the centre, surrounded by four stars – two white ones *above* the crown, and two red ones *below* it. As it was, the white stars had been placed on one side, and the red stars on the other.

'Cut a piece out and sew it back in so that the stars are in their proper places,' roared the king.

Now the king of Neumania means what he says. When he says 'Cut out *a* piece' he means *one* piece – not two or three pieces, and in Neumania the penalty for disobedience is death.

What was the royal flag-maker to do?

Figure 57

A complaint sometimes levelled against the puzzle fraternity is that it concerns itself with a world of unreality. Why can't we get down to earth for once?

All right then; just for once!

The habitable area of Earth (including the Sahara and the polar fringes) is approximately 53,400,000 square miles, and at the end of 1950 this was accommodating a population of 2,509,800,000. That, of course, was some time ago; the figure is now well over the 3,000 million mark, and by the end of 1987 it is estimated that the population will have swollen to 5,019,600,000. Before the century is out it should have topped the 6,000 million mark.

If this relative rate of increase should continue, in what year shall we attain the gregarious distinction of having only one square yard of the earth's surface for each man, woman, and child in the world?

To save you looking up your tables, the number of square yards in a square mile is 3,097,600.

Such problems usually require what is called logarithmic extrapolation, but this is a book of puzzles not a book of mathematics, so the object here is to spot a simple way of finding the answer – which is a rather surprising and frightening one.

Picture blocks are still favourites with young children in the nursery. You know the sort of thing I mean – a set of wooden cubes with fragments of pictures painted on their sides. Since each cube has six sides it is possible to form six different pictures by putting them together in different orders.

The usual number of blocks in a set is twenty, but sometimes there are only nine, or even four – like a set I saw a small girl packing away the other day.

She tumbled them into their square box haphazardly, and then cried in delight:

'Look! They made a picture all by themselves.'

I glanced at the box which looked something like Fig 58.

'That is unusual,' I said. 'I expect you could put them away a hundred times without that happening.'

On the other hand, I reflected to myself, there are six possible pictures which could appear, so that should shorten the odds a bit. Now I am wondering just what the odds are against some picture (any one of the six will do) accidentally appearing complete when the four blocks are packed away. It doesn't matter whether the picture appears upside down or not, or on its side. So long as it is a complete picture with all four blocks in their proper relative positions, it will do. Can you calculate the odds?

Figure 58

If Peter Piper, the pickled-pepper picker, picks a peck of pickled peppers in half the time that Papa Piper, the pickled pepper-picker, picks a peck of peppers.

And a pickled pepper-picker takes half as long again to pick a peck of peppers as it takes a pickled-pepper picker to pack a peck of pickled peppers.

And a pickled-pepper picker takes half as long again to pick a peck of pickled peppers as it takes a pickled pepper-picker to pack a peck of peppers.

And if a pickled-pepper picker can pack a peck of pickled peppers in twenty minutes less than it takes a pickled pepper-picker to pick and pack a peck of peppers.

How long will it take a pickled-pepper picker to pick and pack a peck of pickled peppers?

(If you should decide to tackle the problem experimentally, great care must be taken to ensure that no unpickled peppers become mixed with the pickled peppers, and that the unpickled picker must remain unpickled, while the pickled picker remains in a constant and steady state of inebriation throughout the whole experiment.)

ANSWERS

(1) Marbling*

The winner now has twelve marbles. At the outset the first speaker must have had five, and the second speaker seven.

(2) Tangled Totals*

The nine numbers should be arranged like this:

```
9   9
  5
7 7 7
  9
5   5
```

(3) Space Freight***

Thermidor should take the items weighing 42, 61, and 77 lb, Black Streak should take 35, 44, 48, and 63 lb, and Woomera 28, 84 and 88 lb. This is the only workable allocation.

(4) Lucky Strike**

Joffy found the nuggets weighing 154, 101, and 17 ounces. As for the others, Jem must have found the 46, 22, and 16 ounce nuggets (totalling 84), and Jake the 19, 13, and 10 ounce nuggets (totalling 42). This is the only possible distribution wherein each man finds three nuggets, and Jem's haul is twice the value of Jake's.

(5) And Their Dogs**

Mr Skipper owned Raffles. Mr Raffles owned Pompey. Mr Towser owned Skipper. Mr Pompey owned Towser.

(6) Fencing***

£13. Assume you were to remove the three sections DA, AB, BC, but leave the four corner posts ABCD standing. Since these four posts are together worth £1, the three sections actually removed must be worth £39, ie, each section is worth £13 – and one such section would exactly fill the gap CD. So the problem can be solved without knowing the actual cost of the railing per foot.

(7) In the Balance*

The blonde weighs 7 stone 6 lb, the brunette 8 stone 8 lb. Since Fido and the blonde weigh the same as the brunette, you could replace the brunette in the top picture by Fido and an extra blonde. The two blondes would weigh 16 lb (ie, Fido's weight) less than the he-man, ie, 14 stone 12 lb. So one blonde must weigh half of this: viz, 7 stone 6 lb, and the brunette 16 lb more.

(8) What Price Your Wits?****

The code word is:

PROFITABLE
1 2 3 4 5 6 7 8 9 0

(9) En Bloc*****

My block must be 6 inches square. Such a block would slice up into $6 \times 6 \times 6 = 216$ small cubes of which 96 are black on one side, 48 black on two sides, 8 black on three sides, and 64 all-white.

(10) Collared**

The real priest is the man in Cell Two. The con-man (who always lies) must be in Cell One, and the card-sharp (who, on this occasion, must also be lying) is in Cell Three.

(11) All Buttoned Up**

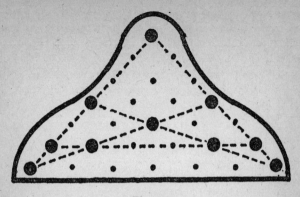

Figure 59

Fig 59 shows how the ten gold buttons should be placed in order to reveal five distinguishable lines of four buttons each.

(12) Tin-snips****

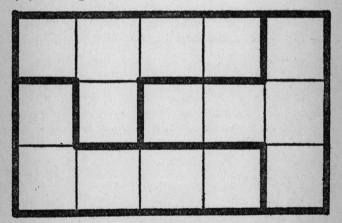

Figure 60

Each of the three pieces shown in Fig 60 can quite easily be folded into a square topless box.

(13) Super Blonde**

I had purchased a can of baked beans and a jar of honey. The prices of the individual items mentioned must have been: Tomato ketchup, 10½p; Sausages, 16½p per lb; Bubblecrisps, 9½p a pkt; Baked beans, 5p; Jar of honey, 19p.

(14) Counted Out*****

The Chancellor should place Gringoli in seat number 2. Whatever total should then be shown on the two dice, Gringoli will inevitably be eliminated at some stage of the count. An indication of how problems of this type may be tackled is given on page 95 of my book *Fifty Observer Braintwisters*.

(15) Tango*

Alex was married to Elizabeth, and partnered Dorothy. Brian was married to Dorothy, and partnered Florence. Charles was married to Florence, and partnered Elizabeth.

(16) Chain Reasoning***

Nineteen links will make ten different triangles, the sides of which will be: 1, 9, 9; 2, 8, 9; 3, 7, 9; 4, 6, 9; 5, 5, 9; 3, 8, 8; 4, 7, 8; 5, 6, 8; 5, 7, 7; 6, 6, 7.

(17) One to Five***

22,412, which equals 431 × 52 (or 52 × 431 if you prefer it that way).

(18) Just for Today****

The statement would be true only if spoken on a Thursday, when last Saturday would be six days away from tomorrow (Friday) and yesterday (Wednesday) would be six days away from next Tuesday.

(19) Wedding Cake*****

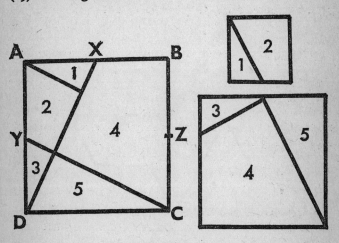

Figure 61

On three sides of the cake mark the mid-points X, Y, Z, as shown in Fig 61. Cut from D to X, and from C to Y. Next, cut from A towards Z, stopping when you reach the first cut. The parts may then be fitted together as shown in the right of the diagram.

(20) Hymn-Board***

Eighty-two cards will be necessary: nine each of 1, 2, 3, 4, 5 and 7, twelve 6s (or 9s), eight 8s, and eight 0s.

(21) Station Sign**

Starting from the S of TRAINS, go round the bottom border to the T, thence along the curved track to the A, and down to the T of TO. From there on you should have no difficulty in tracing out the remainder of the word STATION-MASTER.

(22) Riddle of the Sphinx***

Figure 62

Fig 62 shows how the sphinx may be divided into four minia-ture versions of the original figure.

(23) Wage Claim*

The fivepence-in-the-pound rise is better than the overtime offer. To simplify calculations consider a man on a rate of £1 per hour, ie, £44 per week. Under the overtime scheme he would receive 40 hours @ £1 = £40, plus 4 hours @ £1.50 = £6, ie, £46 all told. But a fivepence-in-the-pound rise would mean 44 hours @ £1.05 = £46.20.

(24) Black Diamond****

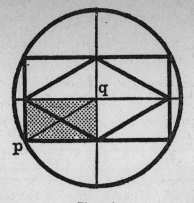

Figure 63

Each side of the diamond is exactly 1 inch long. Draw in the two diameters (vertical and horizontal) as shown in Fig 63. Draw the diagonal *pq* of the small shaded rectangle. Now *pq* is clearly a radius of the circle, so it must be 1 inch long. So the other heavy diagonal of that rectangle must also be 1 inch long – but this *is* one side of the diamond.

(25) Number Please*****

My new number is 8712, which is exactly four times the old number 2178. This is the only possible answer to the problem.

(26) Set-Up****

Sixteen is the smallest possible number of moves. The squares should be moved in this order: S,T,P,S,T,U,E,T,U,P,S,U,P,E,T,P.

(27) Can Be Done*

The only way to score exactly 50 in three shots is to topple first
the 7 on the right-hand pile, then the 8 on the left-hand pile,
and finally the now-exposed 9 on the right-hand pile, giving
$7 + 8 \times 2 + 9 \times 3 = 50$.

(28) Tinker, Tailor ... ***

Anderson is the sailor, Barlow the tailor, Coutts the thief,
Davies the beggarman, Eastley the tinker, and Foley the
soldier. Reading from one end of the street, the house on one
side must be occupied by Barlow, Anderson, Coutts, in that
order, and on the other side by Davies, Foley, Eastley.

(29) Tunnel of Horrors*****

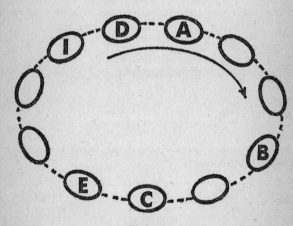

Figure 64

Rusty is Dora's nickname. There must have been eleven cars on
the track with the occupants arranged in the order shown in Fig
64.

(30) Bouquets****

The girls' bouquets were made up as follows:

	Yellow	Pink	White	Red
Alice	5	1	1	1
Barbara	2	1	3	2
Claire	1	1	3	3
Diana	1	4	2	1
Effie	1	3	1	3

(31) Black Mark***

$$289$$
$$764$$
$$\overline{1053}$$

(32) Death Canyon**

(1) A shot D; (2) C shot G; (3) F shot C; (4) B shot F; (5) E shot B; (6) A shot E. Remembering that dead men can't shoot, and that no gunman changed his position, this is the only possible sequence that will account for the six who were killed.

(33) Simply Amazing*****

The only way to thread the maze is to start at the outer circle marked 4, and from there to visit every other 4 in order.

(34) Staff Vacancy****

Only four of the thirty-six girls could do all jobs. (Just for the record, there must have been 5 girls who only typed, 3 who did only shorthand, and 2 with only book-keeping.)

(35) Watered Down****

Fill pot from can. Empty pot into jug. Fill jug with water from tap. Fill pot from jug. Add remaining contents of jug to can. Fill can with water. Both can and pot are now full with a mixture comprising two parts of milk to one of water.

(36) Odd Bits*

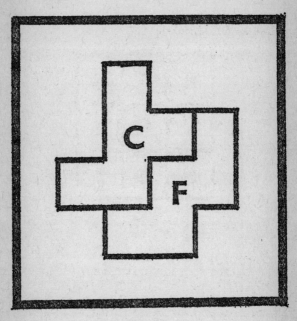

Figure 65

C and F (as shown in Fig 65) are the only two pieces which will fit the hole without being turned over.

(37) Patient Moves***

Ten moves are necessary: A–Emergency, C–4, D–2, B–1, A–3, C–Emergency, D–4, B–2, A–1, C–3.

(38) Outing**

Eighty pence. The price for the original party of thirty people must have been ninety pence per person making the charge for hiring the small bus £27, whereas thirty-five people paying eighty pence each makes the charge for the large bus £28.

(39) Crossnumber Puzzle*****

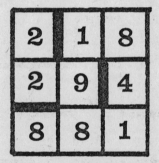

Figure 66

(40) That's Torn It**

The Bath Towel and Face Flannel should cost 25 coupons. Look at it this way; if you were to take up the first and third offers, the total cost would be 50 coupons, for which you would get one of each article. Amongst these, the Hand and Guest Towels (which Barbara does not want) are worth, according to the second offer, 25 coupons, so the remaining two which Barbara does want must also be worth 25 coupons.

(41) Long Division*

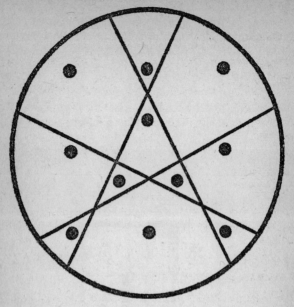

Figure 67

(42) Viewpoints***

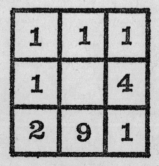

Figure 68

The twenty residents are arranged as shown in Fig 68. So there are 3 who can look North, 12 South, 6 East, and 4 West.

(43) Word-Chains***

1, Only-just-fair-blonde. 2, Autumn-fall-trip-journey. 3, Mark-correct-right-entitlement. 4, Teach-coach-carriage-bearing. 5, Compost-mould-form-class. 6, Jump-spring-season-flavour. 7, Reserve-book-volume-capacity. 8, Dowry-portion-part-role. 9, Decline-refuse-litter-offspring. 10, Shilling-bob-shingle-gravel.

(44) Getting Out of Line*****

If you managed to solve the problem in five moves that is good. Four very good. Three is unbeatable. Here is the only way in which the task can be completed in three moves: A to 1; E to 8; D to 24.

(45) Fathers and Sons****

Bertram Pennywhistle, and his son Edward Pennywhistle. Daffyd Leacock, and his son Archibald Leacock. Edward Massingham, and his son Cecil Massingham. Cecil Norris, and his son Bertram Norris. Archibald Oliphant, and his son Daffyd Oliphant.

(46) Cherchez la Femme*

There are thirty-two different ways of reading 'SHE' – eight starting from the central S, and six starting from each of the other four Ss.

(47) Eeni-Meeni-Myni-Mo**

Victor started counting at L(eonard) calling him 'Eeni'. The children in the ring will then fall out in this order: K,D,A,W,F,L,G,H,Q, leaving V to claim the penny.

(48) Pipe Dream**

10 oz of Mariner's Twist (costing £3.60), and 3 oz each of Blarney's Flake and Three Zeros (costing £1.29 and £1.35 respectively). This is the only combination totalling £6.24 per pound, ie, 39 pence per ounce.

(49) Sum Missing*****

```
              1·008
        _____
6·25)6·3
      625
      ___

      5000
      5000
      ____
      ----
```

(50) Peace Conference****

The only possible combination which will offend no one is: Atlantia, Cornovia, and Empirea (from the Northern powers) with Voolubu, Yubabi, and Zemberia (to represent the Southern *bloc*). There is no need to consult Neumania about it; she will just have to like it or lump it.

(51) Petrol and Paint***

It is useful to know that the volume of any two spherical containers (or for that matter, any two similarly shaped bodies) varies according to the cube of their sizes. Since the new sphere contains eight times as much petrol as the old one, it must be just twice the linear size (because 2^3, ie, $2 \times 2 \times 2 = 8$). Being just twice as large, its *surface area* will be 2^2, ie, $2 \times 2 = 4$ times as much, thus requiring 4 times $20 = 80$ gallons of paint.

(52) Pentominoes*****

Figure 69

(53) Bright and Early*

Bright delivers to eight more houses than Early, irrespective of
how many houses there may be in the street.

(54) Rotas*

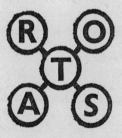

Figure 70

The required letters (shown in Fig 70) make it clear why the
game has been named 'Rotas'.

(55) Flat Out***

Roger and Norma Warren occupy the top flat. Percy and Doris Lewis occupy the middle flat. Jim and Catherine Morton occupy the ground-floor flat. This is the only combination which will account for all the 'ups and downs' of the problem.

(56) Rained Off***

The completed board reads as follows:

	M	Tu	W	Th	F	Tot
A	6	10	2	10	11	39
B	2	13	4	9	7	35
C	4	6	12	12	1	35
D	14	13	8	1	4	40
E	3	5	7	11	3	29
Tot	29	47	33	43	26	178

(57) Economy Cut****

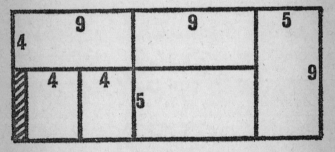

Figure 71

A rectangular piece of laminex 23 inches by 9 inches can be cut as required with a wastage of only 5 square inches. The diagram above shows how it can be done. The shaded area represents the 5 square inch minimum wastage.

DICK HOLLAND   130 COLIN AVE.

(58) Sum Bits and Pieces*****

In Calcularia there are 8 Pieces to the Bit, and 14 Bits to the Sum. On adding the Pieces column one may be tempted to assume that there are 24 Pieces to the Bit, but then the rest of the sum would only work out if we were to assume 13 Bits to the Sum, which is impossible because 13 actually appears in one place in the Bits column.

(59) Treasure Hunt***

A,G,M,D,F,B,R,W,H,P,Z is the only route which enables one to get from A to Z by visiting each village only once.

(60) For Pity's Sake!***

President – Bertie. Chairman – Doris. Vice-chairman – Connie. Secretary – Eve. Treasurer – Albert.

(61) A Dicey Question*****

Reading from left to right, the symbols shown on the reverse sides of the dice are: a Crown, an Anchor, a Heart, and a Club (all pointing downwards).

(62) Not All There**

The pamphlet must originally have contained 14 pages which, had they all been present, would have totalled 105. The leaf bearing page numbers 7 and 8 must have been missing.

(63) Joining Up**

The job can be done for 62½p by cutting all links in the two-link and three-link lengths, and using the resulting five loose links to join the remaining five lengths.

(64) Blankety Blank*

Twenty black squares must be added to the eight already existing, as shown in the Figure below.

Figure 72

(65) The Apple Pie Mystery**

Billy was the culprit so far as the thieving was concerned, but he had told the truth when he said Diane hadn't taken it. Elaine was not guilty of theft but she was the untruthful one.

(66) Roll On***

Twenty-five revolutions. One may be tempted to think that, in travelling a distance of 60 ft, a circle of 2 ft circumference should make 30 revolutions, but not so. The 5-ft roller will make $60 \div 5 = 12$ revolutions, thus the cylinder will circumnavigate the interior 12 times, ie, a distance of $12 \times 50 = 600$ inches, and this will require 25 revolutions of its 2 ft circumference.

(67) Jackpot***

The only set of numbers on the card totalling exactly 100 is: 6,9,15,17,53.

(68) Gun-boat Diplomacy****

Puzzooloo's island is 200 miles in circumference. Both ships set off together. After 40 miles the escort vessel transfers one-half of its remaining fuel to the flagship and returns to port. There it refuels and sails away in the opposite direction to meet the flagship now 40 miles from home, and on its last match-stick. Again the escort vessel transfers one-half of its remaining fuel, and both return to port together, their bunkers being empty upon arrival.

(69) Piece by Piece*
Only one piece need be moved (as shown by the arrow in the Figure below.)

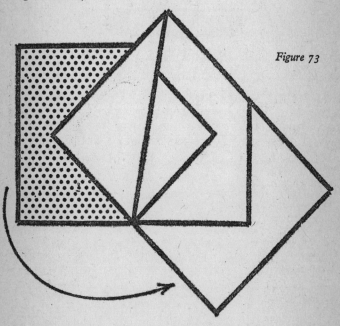

Figure 73

(70) Decanter*****
Turned upside down, the depth of wine in the decanter would

be eight inches. If a flask-diameter shrinks from 24 cm to 2 cm in eleven inches, in twelve inches it will shrink from 24 to zero. So the imaginary cones shown in Fig 74 have heights of $a = 12$, and $b = 10$ inches. Now the volume of wine must equal Cone A minus Cone B, and this must be the same as Cone D minus Cone C (in the inverted picture). But cones of equal slopes have

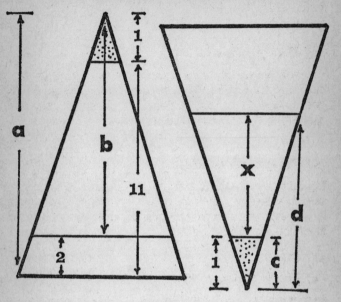

Figure 74

volumes proportional to the cubes of their heights, so $a^3 - b^3 = d^3 - c^3$, ie $d^3 = a^3 - b^3 + c^3$, ie $d^3 = 1728 - 1000 + 1$, ie 729, from which it follows that $d = 9$. Then x must equal $9-1 = 8$. (I hope you didn't get your leg pulled by $0.3937007925984252031496063\ldots$ inches. By using the reasoning shown above, the onerous business of converting centimetres to inches can be side-stepped completely.)

(71) Missing Links*****

Alphalpha, Beetonia and Gammalia are the only towns that can be called from Epsilonna. A is connected to all others, and therefore to E. Now *if* the link B–G does *not* exist, B and G (each with four links) must *each* be connected to A,D,E,Z, which would use up all the terminals of D,E,Z, leaving no terminals in D and Z for the link which we are told does exist. Therefore the link B–G must exist. E must then be connected to both B and G, leaving no terminals in E for any other town.

(72) There's a Twist to It***

You were warned that it was a tricky question with a 'twist' to it, so twist the 6 upside down to make it a 9. Then group the cards 1,2,4,5 (= 12) and 3,7,8,9,9, (= 36). If the 6 is left the right way up the problem cannot be solved.

(73) Eksepshunal Bargins**

I bought the wheelbarrow for £3.05. In the morning Harry must have sold the electric iron and typewriter (total value £3.40) and in the afternoon the painting, the bedstead, and the bike (totalling £6.80).

(74) Cheese Stacking*****

Sixty moves are necessary: 1-b, 2-c, 1-c, 3-b, 1-a, 2-b, 1-b, 4-c, 1-c, 2-a, 1-a, 3-c, 1-b, 2-c, 1-c, 5-b, 1-a, 2-b, 1-b, 3-a, 1-c, 2-a, 1-a, 4-b, 1-b, 2-c, 1-c, 3-b, 1-a, 2-b, 1-b, 6-c, 1-c, 2-a, 1-a, 3-c, 1-b, 2-c, 1-c, 4-a, 1-a, 2-b, 1-b, 3-a, 1-c, 2-a, 1-a, 5-c, 1-c, 2-b, 1-b, 3-c, 1-a, 2-c, 1-c, 4-b, 1-b, 2-a, 1-a, 3-b.

(75) The Glasgow Puzzle**

Eight moves only are necessary. There is nothing in the problem to say which of the two 'Gs' must be used as the initial letter of GLASGOW. If you regard the lower G as the first letter of the word, the problem can be solved by moving the letters in the following order: GASLSAGO.

(76) Think of a Number***

(a) 66; (b) 36; (c) 27; (d) 54; (e) 45; (f) 96 (which, when the digits 2 and 1 are inserted, becomes 9216 which 96 × 96); (g) 39 and 93; (h) 36, 44, or 63; (i) 86 (which, upside down, looks like 98).

(77) Wakey, Wakey*****

We crossed the second arm of the wake at 12.18 PM. When we reached the point where the liner was at noon, we were naturally equidistant from both arms of the widening wake, so from there on it wouldn't really matter which one we chased. If therefore we had turned around, we should have again caught the first arm of the wake (instead of the second arm) just as the first arm reached our original position. By then we should have gone 'there and back' while the first arm was merely going 'there'. This means that the wake's speed was just half our speed. So at 12.06 PM (at which time we first crossed the wake) the wake would need another 12 minutes to cover the distance we had just covered in 6 minutes.

(78) Lock Up**

Grandpa should build another door between the sitting-room and the kitchen. It may seem silly to have two doors between the same two rooms, but there is nothing else for it if Grandpa is determined to pursue his procedure for locking up.

(79) Pentacular Puzzle***

The drawing contains thirty-five triangles.

(80) Just for a Change*

8 tenpenny pieces (worth 80p), 3 fivepenny pieces (worth 15p) and 2 old sixpences (worth 5p) is the only combination of thirteen such coins totalling exactly £1.

(81) Heart Strings*****

The task can be done only by starting at Point X and finishing at Point Y (or vice versa) as shown in the Figure below.

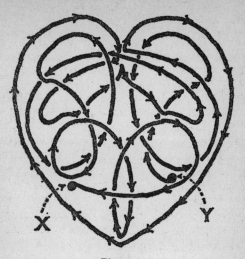

Figure 75

(82) Nuclear Pile**

Three canisters only need be moved. Replace 6 by 3, and 9 by 6, and put the 9 where the 3 was. This gives:

$$
\begin{array}{ccc}
13 & 3 & 14 \\
11 & 10 & 9 \\
6 & 17 & 7 \\
\end{array}
$$

(83) Keeping Track****

(a) No, I cannot say that the average speed was 50 mph. Assume that the distance A-to-C were 120 miles. Then the double 240-mile journey would take $3 + 2 = 5$ hours, making an average speed of 48 mph.

(b) Yes, the average speed on Tuesday from C-to-B was

more than 30 mph. Again assume that A-to-C were 120 miles (though any other distance would do) then C-to-B would be 60. At 30 mph this would take 2 hours, whereas the *whole* journey took only 2 hours, so the speed from C-to-B must have been more than 30 mph.

(c) No, I cannot be certain that I reached B later on Monday than on Tuesday, for the Monday train could have travelled at very high speed to B, and then crawled the rest of the way.

(d) Yes, imagine two aerial movie films, one taken on Monday, and the other on Tuesday, and both showing the whole length of the track continuously in view. If superimposed the films would show the unchanging motionless countryside with two trains crawling towards one another. Clearly they must pass at *some specific spot*, and the time at which they pass this spot must be the same time of day (as recorded for instance on a church clock if such a clock were also part of the scene shown by the synchronized films).

(84) Counting on Annabel***

$A = 2$, $N = 8$, $B = 5$, $E = 7$, $L = 6$, making $288 \times 2 = 576$.

(85) On Time**

24 mph. If 30 mph meant arriving half an hour early, and 20 mph meant arriving half an hour late, the distance can only be 60 miles. At 20 mph this would take three hours, which is half an hour too much. Sir Withers therefore wants to do the journey in $2\frac{1}{2}$ hours, and this will mean travelling at 24 mph.

(86) Round Table**

The seven knights could dine on only three days of the month. Here is a possible seating roster, reading clockwise from Arthur: 1st Day, ABGLMPT (as shown in Fig 50); 2nd Day, AGMTBLP; 3rd Day, ALTGPBM.

(87) Counter-moves***

The diagram shows one solution. Turning the diagram upside down will reveal the other possible solution.

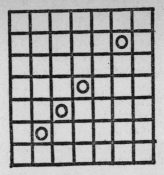

Figure 76

(88) Loss of Water****

It will take twenty minutes for the water to leak from the full tank. Since Tom works only half as fast as Bill, one would expect him to do the job in 8 minutes, but clearly it takes him an *extra* 2 minutes to deal with the *extra* 6 minutes of leakage. In 10 minutes he will therefore put in enough water to leak away in 30 minutes, so the tank will be empty 30 minutes after he starts, ie, 20 minutes after he (or anyone else) has filled it.

(89) Battle of the Sexes (Credits: For guessing correct answer*. For seeing why*****.)

Mother and two boys should beat father and three girls. From the first two pictures, pit the two winning teams against the two losing teams, ie, BBGGGM v FBGGGG. Naturally, the combination of the two strong teams, ie, the left-hand side, will win, and would still win if three girls and a boy were removed from each side. So *BM will beat FG*. Add the third picture to this last result and we have BMFG beating FGGGGM. Take a mother and father from each side, and we can see that two boys will beat four girls, ie, *B will beat GG*. So (combining the two results in italics) BMB will beat FGGG.

139

(90) Stepping It Up***

Twenty seconds. If the escalator takes 30 seconds to cover the distance, it will cover 1/30th of the journey every second. If, on top of this I walk, then I cover 1/12th of the journey every second. My walking therefore accounts for 1/12 minus 1/30 of the journey every second, ie, 1/20th of the journey. So by myself I will complete the whole journey in 20 seconds.

(91) A Dotty Problem**

Eight strokes will suffice as shown in Fig 77.

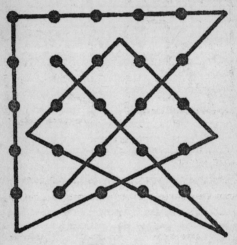

Figure 77

(92) Fitting Numbers***

$$
\begin{array}{r}
54 \\
\times 3 \\
\hline
162 \\
\hline
\end{array}
$$

140

(93) The Darg★★★

When the extra three men have been engaged there will be fifteen on the job. Originally, there must have been ten men each laying 600 a day, then twelve each laying 500 a day. The fifteen will each lay 400 a day. In this way the daily total output remains constant at 6,000 per day.

(94) Table Top★★★★★

The method shown in the diagram below reduces wastage to a minimum, and only two pieces have to be fitted together to form a new table 3 ft × 2 ft.

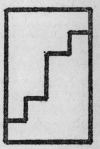

Figure 78

(95) Pawns' Revolt★★

The only possible solution is shown in the diagram below.

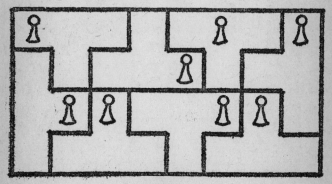

Figure 79

(96) Snail's Pace*****

The snail will descend the wall in one hour exactly. Most people would say 2 3/5th hours, but since the snail slips 3 feet during an hour's rest, it is clear that, for *every* hour spent on the wall, he has to contend with 3 feet of 'slippage'. On a *non-slip* wall he would therefore cover in an hour not a distance of 5 feet, but of 8 feet. During this hour, if he is actively *descending* a *slippery* wall, he will also slip another 3 feet, making a total of 11 feet in one hour – which happens to be the height of our wall.

(97) Flagging****

If the dotted L-shaped piece is cut out and turned over as shown in the diagram below it will fit back with the stars in their proper places, since the motifs on any flag are always visible from both sides.

Figure 80

(98) Close Up, Please!****

At the present rate of increase, the world's population will reach a density of 1 person per square yard in the year AD 2543, ie, in considerably less than 600 years from now. Two facts emerge directly from the data: firstly, in 1950 population density was 47 per square mile; secondly, world population is doubling every 37 years. Thus by 1987 density will have doubled to 94 per square mile, by 2024 to 188 per square mile, and so on. Sixteen such doublings brings us to 3,080,192 per square mile in AD 2542. The number of square yards in a square mile is (as stated in the problem) 3,097,600 – a number which will clearly be reached by the density-figure in the following year, since it represents a further increase of not much more than one-half of one per cent on the 3,080,192 per square mile attained in 2542.

(99) Picture Blocks*****

There is only one chance in 331,776 of some picture appearing. Place the first block arbitrarily in any corner of the box. There is a one-in-four chance that the block will be so placed that an appropriate corner of its picture-piece will correspond with the corner of the box itself. Since three blocks remain to be placed – each with 6 faces, each of which faces may be orientated in 4 ways, there is only 1 chance in $3 \times 6 \times 4 = 72$ of the second placement matching the first. Similarly, the chances of the third and fourth blocks also matching-in are $2 \times 6 \times 4 = 48$, and $1 \times 6 \times 4 = 24$, respectively. The odds against all this happening are therefore $4 \times 72 \times 48 \times 24 = 331,776$.

As a matter of interest, the twenty blocks of a full nursery set are usually arranged in a 5×4 rectangle. The odds against these blocks happening to tumble together to form some sort of picture (either right way up or upside down) are 1 in 81,502,010,850,414,109,487,963,197,493,666,874,654,720, 000. To get some idea of what this number means, imagine that at the time of Creation (say about ten thousand million years ago) each of the present three thousand million people on Earth had been equipped with a set of nursery blocks, and had been working away steadily ever since for 24 hours a day, tossing twenty blocks per second, they would still have about another 85,000,000,000,000,000,000,000 years (or roughly 8,500,000,000,000 *times* as long as the Universe has already existed) before the chances were that one of them managed to get a completed picture.

(100) Pepper Picking*****

It will take a pickled-pepper picker thirty-five minutes to pick and pack a peck of pickled peppers. Suppose Papa *packs* in m minutes; then Peter *picks* in $1\frac{1}{2}m$ minutes; so Papa *picks* in $3m$ minutes; so Peter *packs* in $2m$ minutes, which is 20 minutes less than Papa's time for picking *and* packing, which is $4m$ minutes. So if $4m$ minus $2m$ is 20, then m must be 10, and Peter's time for picking and packing (ie, $1\frac{1}{2}m$ plus $2m$, which is $3\frac{1}{2}m$ altogether) must be 35 minutes.